THE 10 LAWS OF LEARNING

STEVEN RUDOLPH

EBURY PRESS

An imprint of Penguin Random House

EBURY PRESS

USA | Canada | UK | Ireland | Australia
New Zealand | India | South Africa | China | Singapore

Ebury Press is part of the Penguin Random House group of companies whose addresses can be found at global.penguinrandomhouse.com

Published by Penguin Random House India Pvt. Ltd
4th Floor, Capital Tower 1, MG Road,
Gurugram 122 002, Haryana, India

Penguin Random House India

First published by Random House India 2009
Published in Ebury Press by Penguin Random House India 2018

10 9 8 7 6 5 4 3 2

ISBN 9788184000894

Typeset in Sabon by InoSoft Systems, Noida
Printed at Repro India Limited

www.penguin.co.in

FSC www.fsc.org MIX Paper from responsible sources FSC® C047271

This is a legitimate digitally printed version of the book and therefore might not have certain extra finishing on the cover.

For the children of India

Contents

Foreword

The 10 Laws of Learning makes itself indispensable to anyone who is connected to the process of educating children—teachers, principals, parents or even children themselves. In fact, as a one-time housemaster, frequent teacher and principal, and a lifelong learner, I find that this book does a remarkable job of explaining the factors that contribute to a child's success through useful examples, practical suggestions and an engaging style.

Steve and I have spoken about this notion of success many times. For both of us, success is less about the goal—earning a high salary, being the CEO of a large company, running a marathon—but more about the journey. And it is our education that prepares us for this journey.

What is then the goal of education? To my mind, the goals of education are five-fold: First and foremost, education is about realizing our innate potential as human beings. Steve's second law, *teach your children to believe in themselves*, is about discovering and nurturing this potential. We must prepare our children to know themselves, their strengths and their weaknesses, their likes and dislikes, so they are able to make the most of their lives.

Secondly, our education should teach us about the myriad wonders of the world. There is so much in our lives to do, to see, to feel, to hear, to experience and we need to know how to tap into this. We need to teach our children how to celebrate being alive, to appreciate and enjoy each moment and to live life to its fullest. Unfortunately, our schools do not do a very good job of further developing a child's natural curiosity and the sense of wonderment about life and the world around them. And this is where this book comes in handy.

The third purpose of education is again something that Steve touches upon several times through this book: to empower our children to make better choices. I strongly believe that what separates those who have received a good education from those who did not is their ability to take better decisions. When we give children the opportunity to make active choices in their lives, to show them the consequences of both good and bad decisions, it has an incredible impact on their sense of self and ultimately their success.

The fourth goal of education is to teach us to live in coherence with nature. What do I mean by this? Most of our problems today from global warming to the melting of the polar ice caps are a result of leading lives that are in competition with nature. So it is up to us to encourage our children to develop a harmonious and aesthetic relationship with the world around us.

Finally, the fifth purpose of education is to teach us how to be good human beings. According to his holiness the Dalai Lama, a good education system is as much about 'gaining knowledge as about developing basic human qualities'. I strongly believe that one cannot be a good scientist, a good CEO, a good journalist, or indeed a good politician unless one is first a good human being.

I feel these goals can be achieved as much within the walls of a school as outside. Our children today are as much (if not more!) affected by what they see on their way home after school, on TV, what they hear in conversation at the grocery store, or what computer games they play besides what is taught to them at home or at school. And that is a powerful realization. Many of us still believe that education ends when the school is dismissed.

This is far from true! In fact, as a result, we are an over-schooled but an under-educated society.

Steve's book is premised on this very idea—that we are all stakeholders in the process of educating our children and that we can play an active role in helping them become the 'champions' that Steve and I both believe they are!

ARUN KAPUR
DIRECTOR
VASANT VALLEY SCHOOL

Introduction

All parents want the best for their children. They want to see them healthy, happy, and well mannered. And, most of all, they want to see them turn out as achievers. But, parents often feel frustrated in the process of raising children, from infancy to adulthood, constantly searching for the elusive strategy to deal effectively with each problematic situation. They are often left guessing about what to do when their son is unmotivated to study, or when their two children fight incessantly.

Parents tend to draw on past experience—their own upbringing—but at the same time, feel overwhelmed by the complexities of the changed times, a world radically different from what they grew up in. 'What would *my* father have done if *I* kept on chatting online with friends when I should have been studying?' In short, they feel unsure and uncertain whether their parents' methods would still be applicable in an age of satellite TV, computer games, and junk food. Confused, parents turn to books and the Internet to find advice from leading psychologists and experts. However, they often find the solutions to be fragmented, vague, complicated, impersonal or incomplete. When a mother is at the market with her child, who is yelling and crying because he wants a toy he saw in a store window, she doesn't have the time to consult tons of abstract information in order to deal with him.

What parents today need, instead, is a simple set of rules to guide them at every step, so that whatever challenge they may face, they know exactly what to do. These rules have to be *easy to remember* as well as *intuitive*. They also need to be all encompassing, so that they can provide the requisite solution for an over-energetic seven year old, as well as a confused fifteen year old, which is broadly the age group I'm addressing in this book.

After more than two decades in the field of education, working with thousands of children, parents and teachers, and after reading hundreds of books and articles (from the ancient Vedas to the latest studies in neuroscience), I have developed a set of principles which I call the *10 Laws of Learning*. This is what I offer to you in this book. I have derived these Laws from proven, universal principles that have stood the test of time, and have created a simple framework that is both easy to understand and implement. Once you experience the Laws, you will immediately see the beauty of their simplicity, and will easily learn how to use each one of them every time you stumble in the course of raising your children.

THE 10 LAWS OF LEARNING

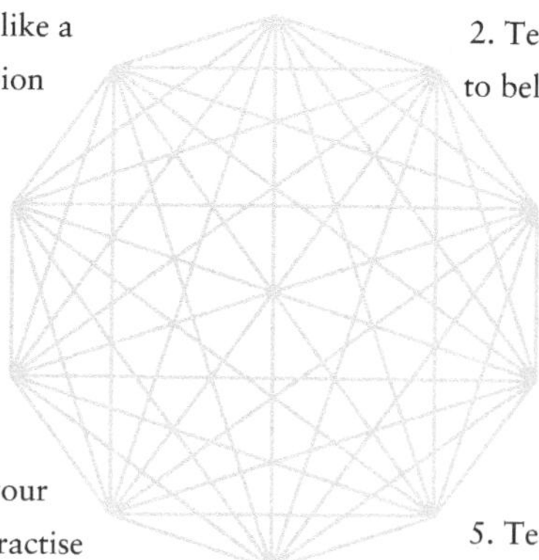

As you look through the *10 Laws of Learning*, you will notice that there is a natural progression that they seem to follow—an order that makes them appear to be logically sequential—(i.e., first you must 'Take care of yourself', then you must 'Believe in yourself', then you must 'Explore your world', then 'Make goals', and so on). However, the laws also have a non-linear relationship (e.g., you need to 'Take care of yourself' while you 'Play'; you need to 'Believe in yourself' while you 'Explore', etc.). The chart above shows the connections between all the 10 Laws.

Coaching

All of us owe a measure of our success to our coaches and mentors. In fact, those who did not become top investors, Olympic winners, or musical sensations will certainly attribute at least some amount of their failure to not having a good coach, the right coach, or any coach at all. As you read through this book, keep in mind that, as a parent, you are the first coach that your child will encounter. And, as a good coach you should:

- Know your 'players' well to bring out the best in them
- Demonstrate commitment and patience
- Be a great motivator
- Be fair
- Know how to be both, soft and tough, depending upon the situation
- Take at least partial responsibility for both, success and failure
- Teach by example (Follow the *10 Laws of Learning* yourself!)

This last point just might be the most crucial of them all. You have to be a role model for your children, as they will ultimately do as you *do*, not just as you *say*. As you go through the book, you might find yourself saying, 'Hey, wait a minute, I have to teach this to my children, yet, I don't do this myself.' Keep in mind that if you don't exercise, don't think your kids will magically do so. If you eat junk food, guess what? Your children will be inclined to eat the same food despite your protests.

How to read this book

You can read this book, chapter by chapter, in the usual way. However, in case you need an instant solution and are hard pressed for time, you can also simply refer to the specific section that is relevant to you. In order to make the sequence and cross-connections between the Laws apparent, I have included references within each chapter to other chapters and sections, which you can follow as they arise, or when you get to them later on. Whichever way you choose to read this book, I am sure you will find it equally enjoyable and beneficial!

Features in this book

As you read through the book, you will find special information to help you in understanding and implementing the 10 Laws better.

- Case Studies: These contain real life scenarios that I encountered as an educator over the years while counselling parents*.
- Coaching Tips: These boxes contain practical, useful ideas for you to strengthen your coaching technique. (*Hey, even coaches need coaching!*)
- Troubleshooting: A list of 25 most common problems that parents face with practical tried and tested solutions.

* All names have been changed to protect the identity of the people involved.

Applying the 10 Laws!

Keep in mind that the 10 Laws are a way of life. Rather than trying to apply all the Laws at once, start with a few that are most relevant to your situation, and then gradually move on to the other Laws.

A friend of mine told me that once he bought a book on parenting to help deal with his five year old son's behavioural problems. He frequently discussed the techniques suggested in the book with his wife, not realizing that his son was listening in on their conversations. One day, his son pulled the plug out from his computer. When my friend asked him why he did that, his son replied, 'I'm teaching you how to handle me.' So be sure to share the Laws with your children openly—it should be something you do *with* them, not *to* them.

Kids today have become quite knowledgeable due to the exposure to the Internet and TV, and can get resentful when parents wield authority without providing logic, or when adults pretend to have everything under control when they are obviously themselves scrambling for answers. Hence, an air of candidness about your own personal development, combined with a sense of fairness and wisdom from your years of experience, will create an ideal recipe for parenting.

Lastly, as you put the Laws into practice, keep your eyes open for innovative ways to improvise, depending on what your child responds to best. You have my whole-hearted support to develop new techniques that help you personalize the Laws, and make them more meaningful for your child. And, if you do discover something you think would be of value and interest to others, please share it with us on our website: http://www.lawsoflearning.com.

STEVEN RUDOLPH
JULY, 2009

Law No. 1
Teach your children to care for themselves

I recently went on vacation to a hill station in North India. There, I met a family with a six year old daughter who was extremely hyperactive and poorly behaved. Before a meal, she managed to convince her parents or grandparents to give her junk food—chocolate, biscuits, chips and other such delights, complaining about how hungry she was, sometimes even throwing a tantrum. By the time the food was served, she would have polished off the junk food, and would then refuse to eat the chapattis, dal, or vegetables, saying she was too full. While I was extremely surprised at the parents' willingness to support her junk food habit, I got the shock of my life when they caved in to her demand for a cold drink one morning before breakfast at 7:45 am!

When the parents discovered that I was an educational counsellor, they immediately hurled a barrage of complaints about their child towards me: 'She's disrespectful, she's destructive, she talks back to us, she never listens'—and, of course—'she doesn't eat properly. What should we do?' They seemed to be totally unaware that they were pumping their child with processed foods which were high in sugar content, and that these were contributing towards her problems. What's worse, their indulgence could have caused a condition of childhood diabetes within a few years.

One of the greatest challenges parents face today is teaching their children to take proper care of themselves. Today's lifestyle has become unnatural in many ways, and its negative impact has wreaked havoc on children's health, often resulting in serious behavioural problems. Although most parents recognize that their children are not leading healthy lives and have developed poor personal habits, they are unsure of how to begin fixing things. In this chapter, I shall address five key life-balancing practices related to eating, breathing, exercise, rest and relaxation, and hygiene, which will help your children to feel positive, energetic, enthusiastic, and as a result, be better learners.

Eating

The junk food crisis

Today, we see food more as a tool to entertain our taste buds than as a source of nutrition that gives us energy to work, play, and live. Day in and day out, we are bombarded by scores of advertisements—on TV and on hoardings—displaying cheap foods filled with sugar, white flour (maida), artificial colours and preservatives. While they have almost no nutritive value, their attractive packaging, tongue-tantalizing flavours, and celebrity endorsements create a temptation that no vulnerable child can resist.

If you are like most parents, you are concerned about your child eating foods which are not healthy. And you're right! Not only are they bad for your child's health, they also inhibit his learning process.

Sugar, you're too sweet!

Kids crave sugar in any form—in candies, biscuits, drinks, and so on. And that's no surprise: sugar is like rocket fuel for our body, getting instantly absorbed into the blood stream. Along with a big dose of sugar comes a 'sugar high'—a physical rush that wakes us up and makes us feel like a superhero. However, our bodies weren't made for such high concentrations of sugar. Whenever your child eats refined sugar, the sugar content in the blood shoots up so much that it sends out an alarm. The body goes into shock and reacts by saying, 'There's too much sugar in the bloodstream. We've got to get it out.' The pancreas then kicks into gear, releasing insulin into the bloodstream, which removes the excess sugar from the blood and stores it as fat.

There are two negative effects of this. The first is that during the process of removing the excess sugar in the blood, the sugar or energy levels drop so much that there is actually too little sugar left in the blood. The child then feels a 'crash'—a drop in energy. Concentration levels also fall, impeding the ability to learn or study. Children then try to boost their energy level by going for another sugar hit, and a vicious cycle sets into motion—almost like an addiction. Repeated bouts of sugar highs and lows are responsible for negatively affecting the pancreas, and can result in childhood diabetes. Secondly, every time the insulin yanks the sugar out of the blood stream and stores it as fat, it ends up creating fat deposits in the body, which directly leads to children becoming overweight, physically inactive, and mentally sluggish.

While it is not easy to eliminate refined sugar completely from your child's diet, you can certainly put some constraints on it. Fruits contain natural sugars in them, which can satisfy a sweet tooth without boosting the glucose levels to very high levels.

Say 'No' to white flour and deep-fried food

Biscuits, crackers, white bread, pizza, and certain pastas, are made from white flour. Do your best to limit their consumption as much as possible. Instead, switch to whole wheat (atta) products as they don't turn into glucose so quickly.

Anytime you deep fry something in oil, the high temperature ends up killing most of the nutrients in the food. So, chips and other fried delicacies are essentially lifeless. Why eat things that won't give you 'life'?

The second thing you have to watch out for is hydrogenated oil, a product found in biscuits and various snack foods. In order to increase the shelf life of packaged foods, the food companies infuse hydrogen into the oil. Hydrogenated oil (also known as transfat) is extremely difficult for the body to break down and ends up increasing bad cholesterol, which gets stored in the fat cells of the body. It is believed that, over time, excessive build up of transfats leads to hardened arteries, strokes, and cancer.

Coaching tip: Read the grocery packets with your kids, and teach them to recognize the harmful ingredients in products to cut out or reduce the intake of hydrogenated oils.

Additives that subtract

There are certain additives in foods that you need to be very careful of, as they wreak havoc on your children's systems. Artificial flavours, colours, and preservatives are added to food items like candies, sauces, soft drinks, etc. to make them look and taste better for a longer time. However, they are linked to all types of health problems including allergies, hyperactivity, asthma, rashes, eczema, damaged kidneys, high blood pressure, and even cancer. Monosodium glutamate (MSG), a flavour enhancer (E621) found in certain chips, soup packets, and fast food items causes overwork of brain cells, leading to their burn out, and subsequent death. It also causes dehydration. Aspartame is an artificial sweetener used to replace sugar, and is commonly found in diet drinks, low calorie foods, and certain vitamins. Aspartame is known to cause damage to the nervous system and can lead to epilepsy, multiple sclerosis, Alzheimer's disease, coma, and even death.

Cold drinks can leave you in the cold

Most cold drinks contain high amounts of sugar,

preservatives and artificial colouring. Buying an inexpensive juicer is a better option. Let your children experiment by choosing their favourite fruits and vegetables and taking out their juice. A single glass of your own home-made natural fruit or vegetable juice can cost half the amount of a typical cold drink!

How to junk the junk food

The key to dealing with junk food is to be strict and consistent—there is no other way. Set the rules, and then enforce them. It is only a matter of perseverance, and if you stick it out, you will emerge the winner and your kids will eat healthier. You will also need the support of others in the family—your spouse, grandparents, uncles and aunts, etc. Explain to them your goals as well as the rules you are implementing, and ask them to not give in to the child's demands. Just be sure not to let up after a few days or weeks. Here are some other tricks.

Get them to go nuts

Nuts are probably one of the best bets in terms of healthy snacks—especially almonds and walnuts. They give instant energy and also contain vitamins A, C, and E, which are good for the brain. Dry fruits such as dates, raisins, and figs are also excellent sources of instant *natural* energy.

I've found that just about all kids love nuts as well as dry fruits. However, they are rarely available to them when they are in the mood for a snack. My suggestion is to buy a bunch of different types of nuts and dry fruits, and stuff them in your kids' pockets before they go to school. The moment they get hungry, they will automatically reach for these natural goodies, and will unwittingly energize themselves in a healthy manner. You can involve your kids in the process by letting them pick the nuts and dry fruits they want each day, and in the proportion that they would like. However, don't let your children overeat them, as they have high caloric content. Usually, a handful at one time is sufficient.

> **Coaching tip:** Try soaking nuts and dry fruits in water first. This is a healthier way to eat them as it makes them more digestible, and prevents them from causing dehydration.

Plan ahead

Keep in mind that *you* are the one who decides which foods your child is exposed to. Plan ahead by ensuring there are plenty of fresh fruits, dry fruits, nuts, and other wholesome things around to eat. If you go to the cinema, a picnic or on a long trip, be sure to carry your own healthy snacks or drinks wherever possible. When you are out, there is a strong likelihood that when your kids are hungry, you might only find junk food available, and might be forced to let them eat it.

Make menus

Children often don't realize the effort and planning that goes on behind the scenes for the food that arrives on the table. It's easy for them to be critical and protest, 'Oh, not spinach again!' when they have so little at stake. One thing you can do to increase their interest in the food is to involve them in preparing weekly menus with you. Creating menus of their choice not only helps build their planning skills, but also ensures that they get to eat what they want. And if they complain later on about not liking what you've made, you can point out that it was their choice after all!

Take your children grocery shopping

The next time you go shopping for food items to the local vegetable market, grocery store or the supermarket, take your children with you and let them actively participate in the whole process. It will not only increase their curiosity, but will also acquaint them with the different food items. Why not let them handle the money and pay for the purchases? This will strengthen their mathematical skills and teach them about budgeting. Finally, depending on their age and ability, let them carry the shopping bags. All in all, involving children in this exercise, teaches them valuable lessons in responsibility, besides being an overall enriching experience.

Cook with your children

Give your kids small responsibilities in preparing food that is age appropriate—anything from cleaning vegetables to mixing raitas. Their involvement need not be laborious or time consuming. When they participate in the food preparation process, they handle the ingredients more intimately, and will be more likely to give new recipes a try or despised ones a second chance.

Lay the table together

Rather than letting children constantly be on the receiving end of all your cooking efforts, have them participate in laying the table or serving your delicacies to other family members (this includes *boys* as well as girls!). Not only does serving foster a sense of giving, it also creates a sense of ownership that leads children to feel a deeper connection with the food and the family.

Saying grace or a small pre-meal prayer

Before the start of a meal, encourage children to express their gratitude for their food rather than just jumping in to satisfy their hunger. Whether said as a prayer to God, or as a thought of appreciation for having sufficient food when others might not be so lucky, a word of gratitude might inspire them to tolerate tastes that don't necessarily tickle their taste buds like junk food do, but which, nonetheless, are good for health.

Call your food names
Here's another great tip to get finicky eaters to eat with relish: try giving fun names to foods. A recent experiment done with pre-primary school children showed that when vegetables were labelled 'X-ray Vision Carrots', 'Tomato Bursts', 'Power Peas', or 'Dinosaur Broccoli Trees', they ate nearly twice as much as on days when the food items went by their normal names. The results seem to indicate that entertaining names make children believe that food will be more fun to eat.

Hold on to your purse strings
Children often use their pocket money for purchasing foods that are not healthy. If you do give pocket money to your kids, have rules about how they are allowed to spend it, putting limits on the type or amount of foods they can purchase. Also, make them accountable for the way they spend this money. See that the allowance is increased or decreased depending on whether or not the spending rules are followed (See Chapter 6 for more on pocket money).

Crack down on the canteen
School canteens are notorious for being the biggest suppliers of junk food to children. Talk to the principal and canteen operators to get them to offer healthier snacks like fruit chaat, fresh fruits, dry fruits, nuts, popcorn, natural juices, lassi, milk, coconut water, etc. We've done this at Jiva Public School, so I can guarantee that it is possible!

Put a limit on junk food
If you feel it is impossible to remove all junk food from your children's diet, make some rules. For instance, tell

them that they are allowed only one item of junk food per day. If they have a cold drink, they cannot have a candy bar. Or, if they have a packet of chips, they cannot also have a packet of biscuits on the same day. Additionally, engage them in jointly making the rules (see page 86 in Rules Chapter).

Eat on time at fixed times

Our body is made up of different systems that work in synchronization with each other. When they get into a rhythm, our bodies feel good. However, when the systems are out of sync, we run into health problems. It is, therefore, important that children learn to eat regularly and at fixed times.

First, they should never skip meals. Sometimes, children are a bit sleepy in the morning and don't feel hungry. But then, after an hour or two, their hunger begins to surge, and they desperately look for something to eat. They usually find some type of junk food to appease their growling tummies whereas others eat the food that was supposed to be their lunch. Then at lunchtime, they have nothing left, and they're still hungry, so they eat junk food again. To prevent this vicious cycle from happening, ensure your children eat a fairly large breakfast before leaving for school. They will need that energy to last them all morning till lunch break.

Dinner should be eaten two hours before sleeping. It is not advisable for kids to eat late and then go to sleep immediately afterwards.

Ensure that your children eat their meals at fixed times. This enables their bodies to get into a set pattern and also prevents the problem of constipation. When children get constipated, excess stool remains in the body. The stool contains toxins, which are reabsorbed into the blood stream and travel to different parts of the body, including the brain. This dulls the function of the brain and even causes headaches. According to Ayurveda, all of us should pass stool every morning to ensure that our system is cleaning itself properly and our mind is at its sharpest.

What to do if your child is not a natural milk guzzler?
We all know that milk is great for growing kids. It doesn't just have calcium for developing bones but also contains vitamins A and D, and a protein called calapin which helps us to communicate better. But, how many Indian children have you met that love their milk? Here are some tips to get your little one pick milk over some nutrition deficient junk food:

- Put some drink mix, such as drinking chocolate, in their glass of milk. Then, slowly reduce the amount as they get used to the taste.
- Ensure they eat other dairy products such as yogurt, lassi (buttermilk) or paneer (cottage cheese).
- Make milk shakes. Try blending in ice along with fruits that your child prefers, like bananas, mangoes, strawberries, etc.
- Give them hot chocolate, as kids usually love chocolate. Try using semi-sweet chocolate to make it, and go easy on the sugar.
- Let breakfast consist of milk mixed into cold cereals, hot cereals and oatmeal. Choose from a variety of cereals available in the market, especially in shapes of animals, toys, etc., which appeal strongly to children.
- Many desserts contain milk, including rice pudding (kheer), ice cream, and fruit cream. Of course, such foods should be offered within limits and once in a while.

- Involve your kids in the process of choosing and making their alternative milk drinks. By being active participants, they'll be more likely to give it a try.

Meditate on munching

It has become a common habit for people to snack on junk food while doing other things, such as having discussions or watching TV. Eating while your attention is focused on something else creates digestion problems that affect both, health and learning. Your stomach needs blood to digest food. But when that blood is diverted to the brain in order to focus on the TV or the conversation on hand, the food gets poorly digested. Being thus distracted, you might not realize when you are full, so you might have the tendency to overeat or undereat.

Teach your children the importance of focusing on their food while eating—of treating it as a *type of meditation.* It enables them to digest their food better and get more energy from the food. Here are my ten rules for eating which you can share with your kids:

1. Wash your hands before eating.
2. Eat in a quiet place.
3. Say a prayer or thought of gratitude before eating.
4. Avoid talking or watching TV during meals.
5. Look at what you are eating and try to relish each bite.
6. Ensure you chew every mouthful slowly and carefully.
7. Take on your plate only what you can finish.
8. Leave a little room in your stomach. Don't stuff it to the brim.
9. Rinse your mouth after eating.
10. Rest for 20 minutes after eating to let your food get digested.

People need to water themselves too

Water is one of the best sources to boost all areas of your child's life. If there was one top recommendation I had to make, it would be for children to drink more water. Water oxygenates your brain cells and cleans out the toxins from the body, making all the systems work better. If you are feeling sleepy, it can even wake you up! It also aids in digestion, enabling you to get more energy out of the food you eat.

> **Coaching tip:** Ensure that your children drink at least 8–10 glasses of water per day. In summers, and when they exercise, they will need more.

Children frequently don't realize that they are not drinking enough water. They get so involved and engaged in various activities that they often forget to drink water, causing their bodies to dehydrate. In the process, the blood thickens and less oxygen reaches the brain, resulting in, among other things, a lack of ability to concentrate and to study. Not drinking enough water also leads to constipation.

To ensure your children are drinking lots of water, make sure they keep a bottle of water by their side at all times. Keep doing water checks with them. You can even put up a poster or chart that reminds them to do so: *Drink More Water!*

Drinking lots of water will naturally make your children pass urine more frequently. It will also make the colour of their urine clear. This is a good sign, as it indicates that the toxins are being adequately flushed out. Tell them that if the colour of their urine is dark yellow, and if it has a strong odour, it is a warning that they are not drinking enough water.

Exercise is as important as breathing

Don't kids already know how to breathe?

While breathing is critical for survival, there is also such a thing as proper and improper breathing. You can blame that on our unnatural lifestyles—sitting in chairs, hunching over desks, and working on computers are activities that the body was not designed to do. As a result, our breathing has become much more shallow, restricting oxygen from getting into the lungs, and thus to our brain and other parts of our body. Improper breathing also increases stress and weakens the immune system.

When teaching proper breathing, the first step is getting your kids to breathe through their noses. The second part is to get them to breathe from their stomachs rather than from their chests. If you've ever watched infants sleeping, you'll notice that their stomachs go up and down when they breathe as they demonstrate perfect breathing techniques!

Game for the breathing test?

Want to see what I mean? Here's a challenge: Go ahead right now and take a deep breath. A huge, deep breath...

Did you see your chest expand? If yes, then you are among those who have developed an improper breathing technique. Try it again, this time ensuring your chest doesn't move, but that your stomach expands as you breathe in, and contracts when you breathe out. It should feel like a balloon inflating as it sucks in air and deflating as the air is released. (It's not as easy as it sounds! If you need some help, try putting your hand on your navel. Slowly ease your hand away and ensure your stomach follows it.)

What happens when you breathe this way is that the stomach expands outwards, causing your intestines and other innards to move out of the way, and to make room for the diaphragm to pull the lungs down to their fullest capacity. As a result, you get the largest breath of air possible. More air in the lungs means more oxygen in the blood stream, which means, more oxygen going to the body parts and brain, and ultimately, better brain performance.

Deep breathing has many implications for learning. One is that it can control nervousness. When people are under stress (e.g., they have to give a test or speak in front of an audience), they become tense, and start taking shallow breaths from the chest. The lack of oxygen teams up with the psychological fear factor, robbing the brain of oxygen, and cutting off the mind's access to the cerebral cortex (the seat of long term memory). You might recall a time where you had to give a speech or take a test, and your mind went blank. That's what was going on!

In future, whenever your children are in a situation where they need to perform cognitively, and they feel stressed, tense, or nervous, get them to shift their attention to their breathing. Encourage them to take deep breaths from their stomachs—slowly and rhythmically. Within a few breaths, the tension will ease and clarity of thought will return. Try it—it's not so hard. In fact, even a baby can do it!

Wise up to exercise

You must have heard that exercise is good for you and your children. But, you might not realize how *much* of an impact it can have on your children—on their health, as well as on their academic performance. Mothers are in a constant struggle to keep their children from falling sick. Did you know that kids who exercise regularly are less prone to allergies and colds, and miss fewer school days? They are also less likely to become overweight and to develop diseases such as diabetes. The increase in blood flow due to aerobic activity pumps more oxygen and nutrients throughout the body, and especially to the brain. It also eliminates toxins and waste, giving children a fresh, energetic feeling. It is no wonder that exercise increases the abilities of concentration and memorization.

Further, many children suffer from stress due to continuous academic pressure, and by being cooped up indoors, studying for the majority of their day. Nature has provided us with a natural stress buster in the form of exercise, which releases endorphins (the body's feel-good chemicals), and reduces anxiety and depression. Parents are often perplexed about why their kids are moody, and, unfortunately, turn to psychologists and drugs when all that's required to lift their spirits is a daily dose of romping around outside.

So, be sure that your children spend at least one hour daily, doing some type of strong physical activity (two hours for pre-schoolers). In Chapter 8, you'll learn more about the power of *play*, which is directly connected to the benefits of exercise. But for now, suffice it to say that exercise can consist of any type of activity that gets the lungs and heart pumping—skipping rope, cricket, badminton, football, dancing, swimming, skating, running, tennis—there is no end to the list of ways to exercise. Just find the ones that your kids enjoy the most and that'll do the trick.

> **Coaching tip:** Exercise is not just beneficial for your kids. It's also critical for you. If you get involved in physical activity along with them, you'll inspire them to make exercise a regular part of their lives—just like brushing their teeth and bathing.

Case study

A woman who runs a health club in Delhi came to meet me with her fifteen year old son, Vivek, who had not been doing well in school. Apart from studies, he used to spend most of his time either watching TV or surfing the Internet. As a result of his sedentary lifestyle, the boy was overweight and his face was covered with pimples, causing him to be withdrawn and depressed. The woman was worried about her son's situation—his health, his grades, his appearance. But, she was also worried because of the comments that others made about her running a health club and having such an unhealthy-looking son.

After speaking with her son, I found out that neither was he very competitive by nature (he did not enjoy playing team sports) nor did the idea of working out at the gym appeal to him. He eventually revealed a personal interest in dance. So I convinced his mother to enrol him in a dance programme after school. This was like a complete awakening for him—you cannot imagine the sense of joy he got from this activity. Within a few weeks, his long hours before the TV were replaced with a good two hours a day at the dance studio. Not surprisingly, he lost weight, his skin cleared up, and his level of self-confidence increased. To top it off, his grades shot up. Though he still has not developed an interest to spend time at his mother's club, she doesn't seem to mind, as he has achieved what she had hoped for—a healthy, happy son, and an end to the unkind remarks about both of them.

Stretching it out

Due to our somewhat unnatural lifestyles, our bodies get contorted into strange positions that they were never intended to be in, resulting in the muscles getting constricted and the blood flow slowing down. As a result, less oxygen gets distributed throughout our bodies to the trillions of cells that await their life-sustaining fuel. Teaching your children to stretch regularly is a practice that will benefit them immensely in their school-going years—and into their adult lives as well. It removes sleepiness, increases concentration, and reduces stress and tension.

Yoga Power

Simple, basic stretches that can be done any time:

1. Stretching the arms up to the sky
2. Touching the ears to the shoulders
3. Head rolls
4. Twisting the torso
5. Clasping the hands behind the back and looking up
6. Touching the toes
7. Standing on the toes

Our bodies need rest too!

Sleep and rest are intrinsic to the learning process. Some children believe that by increasing study time, they'll be able to learn more. But the fact is, as in many cases, there are diminishing returns on certain investments—and studying is one of them.

During the process of studying, the brain is busy acquiring new information, releasing various types of neurotransmitters. Rest provides the brain with time to shuffle and organize new information, as well as stock up on and create fresh supplies of neurotransmitters. Think back upon your own school days. When you pushed yourself to study more and more, after a certain point, didn't your brain start to feel fuzzy and saturated? But when you got some rest or some sleep, you felt fresh afterwards.

Case study

Once Rahul, a student of Class 9, asked me how to remember what he was studying. He explained that he was studying about eight hours per day outside of school hours, and was getting about 5–6 hours of sleep per night.

I advised him to reduce his study time by 2–3 hours, and increase sleep time by the same amount. Within a few days, he noticed improvements in his concentration levels, and after a few weeks, there were significant improvements in his memory as well as his performance in school.

How much sleep is right?

Here is a chart to let you know approximately how much sleep your child should be getting each night:

Age	Required hours of sleep
12 months old	14.5 hours
2 years old	13 hours
5 years old	11 hours
10 years old	10 hours
16 years old	8.5 hours

Coaching tip: While longer naps of more than one hour are all right for younger children, older children (above six years) should avoid sleeping during the day as far as possible.

Case Study

Recently, a mother and father came to me with their six year old son, Aryan, complaining about his poor behaviour and lack of concentration in studies. Over the past few months, he had become violent and uncooperative, and they could not figure out what was causing this change in his behaviour. Further inquiries revealed that his father had a new job assignment for which he had been working late, returning home daily at 10:30 pm. His son, accustomed to spending time with his father in the evenings, forced himself to stay awake until his father's return. He would then eat dinner with him, and go to sleep between 11:30 pm and midnight. Next morning, his mother would wake him at 6:00 am to get ready for school.

To me, the reason for this behaviour was very clear: he wasn't getting enough sleep. I convinced the father to get home earlier, and ensure that his son got at least 8.5–10 hours of sleep. After doing so, the son's behaviour and concentration problems immediately vanished.

Here are ten tips to sleep well:

1. Don't let them watch TV just before going to bed.
2. Ensure they finish eating dinner at least two hours before sleeping.
3. Maintain a regular sleeping schedule.
4. Make sure the room they sleep in is completely dark.
5. Have them wear loose, comfortable clothes while sleeping.
6. If they can't fall asleep, have them drink a glass of warm milk.
7. Don't let them eat products containing sugar or white flour before they sleep as it will increase blood glucose and may keep them awake.
8. Don't let them have beverages at night that contain caffeine, which can prevent them from falling asleep.
9. Try to encourage them not to nap in the day time. However, if they feel sleepy in the day time, don't let them nap for more than 20 minutes. Otherwise, they will fall into deep sleep and feel groggy when you wake them.

10. Encourage them to create a relaxation routine before going to bed. This could include reading, taking a warm bath, reading a book, or listening to soothing music.

High on hygiene

On more than one occasion, I have walked into a school classroom and almost fainted due to the strong body odour emanating from the room. On such days, I wonder what parents are teaching their children about hygiene. The fact is simple: no one likes to be in close proximity to someone who smells bad or looks dirty. You can improve your children's chances of being accepted among their classmates and teachers by teaching them some simple habits about personal grooming. Read on to discover five tips about personal grooming that even kids should know:

1. Change clothes regularly

As children are physically active, they tend to sweat quite a bit. Ensure they change their clothes regularly, and that underclothes, including socks are changed *daily*. School uniforms should be taken off as soon as your children come home from school; have two sets of school uniforms so that your child can wear a freshly-washed set daily.

2. Air your shoes and feet

Keep a separate pair of shoes for school, and ensure your child removes them after returning home, so that the odour disappears by next morning. Ensure that the shoes and socks are washed regularly. Make sure your kids wash their feet daily, and that they dry the toes and the spaces between them carefully (that's where lots of bacteria collect and turn into that awful foot odour!). They can also use foot powder inside their shoes to absorb sweat and avoid unpleasant smells.

3. Bathe regularly, especially in summer

Once your children reach the age of twelve or thirteen, their sweat will begin to smell unpleasant due to hormones released during puberty, especially during summer. Encourage them to bathe regularly, and use anti-bacterial powder or mild anti-perspirants under their armpits.

4. Hair care

Ensure that your child shampoos her hair regularly to remove the dead skin cells and dirt from the hair and scalp. To keep hair lustrous and smelling good, a regular scalp massage with natural oils is a must.

5. Brush teeth twice a day

Make sure your kids brush their teeth twice a day—once, after waking up, and again, before going to bed. Encourage them to floss their teeth every night before they brush their teeth. Also, ensure they rinse their mouths with water after eating anything.

> **Coaching tip:** Hygiene need not be a dull and boring topic. I created a cartoon character named 'Hi-Genie' whom you can introduce to your children to make the topic of hygiene fun! You can find her at: www.jiva.com/hi-genie.

The Ayurvedic approach to cleaning

This approach pushes us to go beyond merely waking up, mindlessly brushing our teeth and taking a shower. Here, the morning routine is transformed into a deeper life practice. Let your children follow this approach. They will begin to recognize themselves as sentient beings, who interact with the world through five channels, all of which need to be taken care of so that they operate at peak performance. These are:

1. **The Eyes:** After waking, have your children splash water into their eyes.

2. **The Nose:** Ask them to blow out gently from the nostrils. Also, before sleeping they can put a drop or two of almond oil in each nostril and inhale it deeply. This lubricates the nasal passage and pacifies olfactory nerves.
3. **The Tongue:** After brushing their teeth, they can clean the tongue by using a tongue scraper. This removes toxins (ama) coating the tongue.
4. **The Ears:** At night, they can take a cotton ball soaked in sesame or mustard oil, put it in their ears and leave it overnight. Next morning, they can clean their ears gently with an ear bud.
5. **The Skin:** Let children bathe in water that is neither too hot nor too cold. Be sure to use natural, herbal cleansers. Avoid chemical-based products.

Getting kids to tune into themselves

The ultimate aim of this Chapter, and of the first law of learning, is to get kids to take care of themselves. Parents need to go on explaining the fundamentals to them, and reminding them how to stay fit until they finally begin to do so themselves.

One of the ways you can help children to take the step to independence is by introducing them to the Self-O-Meter. I came up with this concept and applied it with my students at Jiva Public School who have found it to be very valuable. I explain to them that we use a thermometer to measure the temperature and a speedometer to measure speed. But, we have nothing to measure how we feel. So, I tell them to imagine that there's a device called a Self-O-Meter that they can use to check on themselves from time to time—to see if they are too hot, too cold, thirsty, hungry, tired, worried, or uncomfortable. The Self-O-Meter would then suggest to them to take the appropriate measure. Thirsty? Drink some water. Sleepy? Take a walk! Uncomfortable? Stretch and change positions, etc.

I've encouraged students at Jiva Public School to try this. Some have even made drawings on pieces of paper, the size of a playing card, and kept it on the desktop. From time to time, when they glance up from their books, they see their Self-O-Meter, figure out the state they are in, and act accordingly to remain balanced. It's a fun way to take care of oneself. Give it a try with your kids!

Short hand

- Teach your kids the five key life-balancing practices related to eating, breathing, exercise, rest and relaxation, and hygiene, which will help them to feel positive, energetic, and enthusiastic.
- Instead of imposing a blanket ban on junk food, make your children understand the drawbacks of food items such as sugar, white flour, deep-fried food, additives, and cold drinks, so that they have genuine reasons for avoiding these items.
- Bring about a favourable change in your children's food habits by giving them healthy food alternatives, explaining their benefits, and making these available on time. This also includes involving them in the process of preparing and serving food.
- You can offer your children a healthy and balanced school life by instilling good habits and lifestyle practices in them such as breathing the right way, blending the right amount of exercise and rest in their routine, and maintaining basic hygiene.

Law No. 2
Teach your children to believe in themselves

Parents come to me everyday with their children, to help them sort out all types of problems. Sometimes, it is a three year old who won't share her toys. Other times, it is a nineteen year old who has failed his board exam twice. But, there is one common issue that I find in just about every instance: children not measuring up to their parents' expectations. While I think it is necessary for parents to expect the most out of their kids, the problem is that they often have misconceptions about their children's abilities, or are unaware of the best ways to help their kids realize their potential.

In this Chapter, I will focus on the three key aspects of getting an accurate understanding of who your kids really are, and to help them develop a strong sense of self-confidence that will lead them to *believe in themselves.*

Understanding your child's nature

Once upon a time, there were three brothers who were farmers. One day, they found a most beautiful seed and went to their field to plant it. The first farmer buried the seed in the ground, but nothing happened. The second brother shouted at him, 'Fool, don't you realize you have to put water on it, otherwise it won't grow.' So this brother brought a jug of water and poured it over the seed. The three brothers waited a few days, but nothing happened. The third brother then scolded the other two, 'In all these years, it seems that both of you have learned nothing about farming. You have to put fertilizer on the seed to make it grow.' So he brought some cow dung, and put it on the ground above the seed. Even after several days nothing happened.

A wise old man, sitting nearby, had been witnessing the entire episode for more than a week. Finally, the old man hobbled over to the three farmers, and asked them, 'What are you doing?' To which the brothers replied, 'We're trying to make this seed grow.' Then the old man asked, 'What kind of seed is it?' The men looked blankly at each other and answered, 'We don't know.' The old man exclaimed in surprise, 'Then, of course, it won't sprout! Every seed is different and needs to be treated differently. First, go and find out what kind of seed it is. Only then will you know how to care for it and make it grow into a beautiful tree.'

The story of the three farmers is very much like the story of most parents I meet. They are so concerned with getting their child to excel in school that they don't even bother to consider what their child's unique qualities are. At the same time, many are interested, but don't know how to go about doing so. Here are a few ways to understand your child's nature:

What is Multiple Intelligences?

Multiple Intelligences is a theory proposed by Howard Gardner, an American educator at Harvard University, who claims that there is more than one kind of intelligence. In fact, he states that there are eight types of intelligences (called Multiple Intelligences, or MIs). These include:

1. **Bodily Intelligence:** the ability to move with grace, use body language effectively, play sports, and understand things through hands-on activities.
2. **Interpersonal Intelligence:** the ability to communicate effectively with others, participate in social gatherings, listen to people attentively and understand their view point, and respect others' feelings.
3. **Logical Intelligence:** the ability to think in numbers and symbols, classify and label things, organize and

sequence things, and ask questions in logical manner.

4. **Linguistic Intelligence:** the ability to read and write well, spell words correctly, discuss and debate effectively, and use quotes, sayings or phrases while speaking or writing.
5. **Visual Intelligence:** the ability to think in pictures and images, to paint, sketch and draw, to create models, and imagine and visualize things.
6. **Musical Intelligence:** the ability to easily learn and play different musical instruments, differentiate between pitch, tone, and rhythm, and recognize different instruments in a song.
7. **Intrapersonal Intelligence:** the ability to spend time alone, express strong beliefs and inner values, discuss life issues, and know one's own strengths and weaknesses.
8. **Naturalistic Intelligence:** the ability to take care of pets and wild animals, collect and organize things, and enjoy spending time being in nature and doing outdoor activities.

It is important to note that your child possesses *all* eight types of intelligences, although in varying proportions. Some intelligences will be stronger than others, which helps to explain why some children do remarkably well with learning languages, but lack the ability to work well with numbers. Or, why some may be gifted athletes although their socializing skills are weak.

Sometimes parents become concerned because their child lacks in a particular area, and get obsessed with improving that one area while ignoring the others. However, keep in mind that each intelligence has tremendous value in school as well as the workplace, and rather than the parents becoming pre-occupied with why their son struggles in English class (and forcing him to make unreasonable achievements), they would be better off recognizing his other talents and nurturing them. As a life coach for your children, you have the challenge of bringing out the best in them. If you observe a particular talent within your child, you should do everything you can to cultivate it. On the other hand, you should have *reasonable and fair* expectations from your children when you see them lacking in any particular talent.

> **Coaching tip:** The concept of MIs is depicted well in the film Taare Zameen Par. Watch the film with your kids and discuss the strong and weak intelligences in the character of Ishaan.

How to find out your child's MI type?
Now that you know something about Multiple Intelligences, it is time to do some research and find out which MI is dominant within your child by doing a Multiple Intelligence test. MI tests are offered by schools, counsellors and even educational websites. One such site is www.jiva.com/mitest. Though MI tests are not always perfect, they do provide an indication, which is helpful in understanding your child's abilities. It is advisable to take the test every few years, as children are constantly developing, and sometimes certain intelligences become more prominent over time.

Make an 'intelligent' connection
Knowing about your child's MI has another benefit when it comes to learning. You can help your children increase their interest, understanding and ability to remember new topics by connecting their strong intelligences with whatever they are learning. So for instance, if your daughter has strong Visual Intelligence and enjoys drawing, have her learn new topics in history by drawing pictures about

them—or by writing with different colour pencils and sketch pens. If your son has a way with words, encourage him to write a diary or a poem about what he learned in his physics class. Children with strong Logical Intelligence can take topics in social studies and create flow charts, and even equations that depict events in history (e.g., regarding the Allies and Axis Powers in World War II: The US + the UK + the USSR > Germany + Italy + Japan).

Case study

Once, a dejected father of a thirteen year old girl, Simran, came to me seeking help. No matter how much she tried, Simran could not excel in Maths. This was not only affecting her grades, but also her general self-confidence. The parents got worried, not knowing what to do.

I told the father that unreasonably pushing Simran to score superior marks in Maths would most likely not bear much fruit, as her Logical Intelligence might be weak. And worse, being demanding of her in Maths could wind up frustrating her severely. Instead, a better idea would be to have more reasonable expectations in tune with Simran's aptitude, planning for modest grades in Maths, but higher grades in an area where her intelligences are dominant (e.g., Linguistic or Visual). I'm happy to share that Simran's parents consequently stopped pressuring her and became pleased with her much improved performance in English and creative arts—especially painting.

What is Multiple Natures?

Another model that is helpful in understanding your child's qualities is the one that I created called Multiple Natures. Multiple Natures (MN) is a framework that explains what people *do* with their intelligences. I have described below the nine unique natures that exist within every person. In the same way as with MIs, some natures are stronger and some are weaker.

1. **Protective:** the tendency to protect (others, animals, the environment, culture, etc.)
2. **Educative:** the tendency to teach others
3. **Administrative:** the tendency to get work accomplished
4. **Creative:** the tendency to come up with innovative ideas
5. **Healing:** the tendency to help others reach a state of balance and health
6. **Entertaining:** the tendency to amuse others
7. **Providing:** the tendency to serve others
8. **Entrepreneurial:** the tendency to create value and wealth
9. **Adventurous:** the tendency to explore boundaries and push limits

Multiple Natures is especially useful in helping understand which careers are likely to be suitable for your children. For instance, those with a strong Healing Nature would make good doctors, nurses or therapists. However, if they don't have a deep concern for others' health, pushing them into such professions could lead to a lifetime of frustration. At the same time, if you notice that your children have a strong Providing Nature—that they enjoy serving others food or lending them a hand when they need assistance, they might be ideally suited to work in customer-service type of professions (e.g., flight attendants, hotel guest managers, chefs, human resource executives, etc.). Guiding such children to become criminal lawyers (where a Protective Nature is required) would not likely result in career satisfaction.

Coaching tip: Your child has all eight intelligences and all nine natures. The strengths of each one add up to make your child's own unique personality type. The Jiva Career Test (www.jiva.com/careertest) can determine not just their MIs and MNs, but can also suggest careers that are compatible with their particular profiles.

Parents often come to me because they want their children to pursue traditional, 'safe' careers (doctors, lawyers, engineers, accountants, etc.). However, their children have radically different ideas, often wanting to become fashion designers, animators, media professionals, or actors and singers. They ask me to 'talk some sense into them'!

During our session, I don't take the side of either the parent or the child. I simply have the child do an MI and MN test. I then ask the child to see for himself if the natures required for those jobs match with his own nature. Sometimes they do, and sometimes they don't. By analysing his personality with MI and MN, I demonstrate that it is one thing to have strong Musical Intelligence, but quite another thing to have a strong Entertaining Nature. Actors and singers have to perform constantly, and unless the child has an innate tendency to continuously amuse others, he will suffer having to go up on stage—every day, again and again and again... That's not to say that he or she would be better off becoming an engineer. This method eliminates the ego element from the decision-making process, making it more scientific and objective. The key is to find out the child's MIs and MNs and match the job to his profile.

Case study

Three years ago, a financial controller of a large IT company in Chennai came to me regarding his sixteen year old son, Karthik, whom he wanted to become a chartered accountant. In an angry tone, he revealed how the boy's Maths scores were particularly low, and worse, that his son had dreams of becoming a designer.

I made Karthik take an MI test, and thereby determined that although his Logical Intelligence was average, his Visual Intelligence and Creative Natures were particularly high. It became clear to me that the father wanted his son to fulfil his own vision rather than help his child build a career based on his own individual nature. After some discussion, I convinced the father to give things another thought, and to let his son give graphic designing a chance. He agreed. Today, his son is happily studying in one of the top designing schools in India, and has already done professional freelance work.

How can apples be oranges?

I believe that the severe cases of stress that we see in schools nowadays, as well as the outrageously high number of student suicides, is a direct result of parents trying to make apples grow in Kerala and coconut trees grow in Himachal. Or worse still, expecting a pear tree to bear figs. Whichever analogy you prefer to use, the fact remains that your children will be far more successful, happy and balanced in their lives when they know their natures and work in accordance with them.

Case study

A woman from Meerut once came to visit me for consultation regarding her eleven year old daughter, Ankita. A housewife, who had dedicated her entire life to supporting her family, the woman skipped all formalities and got straight to the point: 'She's not a good student. Her sister is much better than her in almost every subject.'

I told her that there was no use comparing apples and oranges. 'I'm sure Ankita has incredible qualities of her own.' The woman agreed, and began to identify her daughter's positive traits. She acknowledged that Ankita had a very strong Providing Nature, and that she was very helpful in serving food, would help her in cleaning, and taking care of the home. The mother went on to describe her daughter's abilities in dancing, singing, telling jokes, mimicry—and how well she got along with others. Within moments, she had her own answer: that both her daughters were different, each gifted in her own way.

Coaching tip: Keep in mind that when you start the comparison game between children, you also inadvertently trigger sibling rivalry and feelings of jealousy. Instead of comparing your children, identify and celebrate their unique abilities.

The knowledge of your children's MIs and MNs is beneficial in:

1. Figuring out which academic and extra-curricular activities they are more suited to,
2. Enhancing learning by involving strong intelligences,
3. Identifying the right stream (academic major),
4. Advising them on the right career and professional path.

Nature or nurture?

Parents frequently ask me, 'Are my children born with these qualities, or can these qualities be developed?' The answer to both questions is 'Yes'. Both, modern scientific research and ancient knowledge, concur that children are born with certain qualities (called guna in Sanskrit). At the same time, environment plays a strong role in enhancing those qualities.

For instance, if a child is born with strong Musical Intelligence and is taught how to play an instrument or gets formal training, then that innate musical ability will get enhanced significantly. Attitude also has tremendous impact. For example, a child who dreams of writing songs that will help end poverty can develop her musical and linguistic abilities—even if she is significantly lacking in these areas—just through sheer dedication to her cause. (We'll learn more about the power of passion in Chapter 3.)

Take your pick

The second part of helping your children develop their self-confidence involves teaching them to make choices. While parents typically enjoy the dependency of their children on them during the early years of childhood, they do, eventually, want to see their kids become independent—to be able to take responsible decisions regarding their studies, their diet and their schedules—without having to be supervised constantly or reminded again and again. Children, too, are keen to get in control of their lives. In fact, when they do things on their own, they feel a sense of accomplishment and pride.

However, in real life, it is usually the parents or teachers who call most of the shots: 'Wake up, wear these clothes, eat this food, read this chapter', and so on. As a result, children have very few opportunities to make important, genuine choices. This has two negative consequences. First, children fail to develop their decision-making skills. Second, when children are constantly forced to comply with others' wishes, they become dependent on others. As they grow up, they constantly seek approval for even the smallest decisions—which tie to wear, which soap to buy, or what to make for dinner. In fact, the decision-making process for some can become a terrifying task!

So my first bit of advice to parents is to *give your children choices*. Whether it relates to schedules, clothing, or entertainment, do your best to let your kids make decisions at every possible juncture. Here are ten everyday choices you can give your children:

1. Toys or games they would like to play with
2. Food they would like to be cooked for dinner
3. The healthy snack they would like to take to school
4. Particular cups, plates and utensils they would like to eat with
5. Clothes they would like to wear
6. Books they would like to read
7. Chores at home they would like to take on
8. TV shows they want to watch
9. The ways in which they would like to decorate rooms in their house
10. Gifts to buy for others on special occasions

Case study

Not long ago, a young couple from Gujarat came to visit me with their bright and energetic five year old son, Dev. They were looking for ways to deal with his stubbornness and anger, which began to surface 15 minutes into our meeting. Unable to stay confined to a chair in an enclosed room, he started running around my room, pulling out several colourful books and games from my bookshelf, with his mother running after him, trying to control what she thought was improper behaviour. The boy's emotions seemed to be wavering and he began pleading with her to go outside to play; much to his parents' discomfiture, his voice began to get louder and louder. Both parents were noticeably frustrated.

Realizing that something needed to be done, I turned to the child and said, 'Dev, it seems like you want to play outside as well as read. I'll give you a choice: you can either play outside with your Mom for 5 minutes and then read, or you can read now and then play outside.' The boy instantly calmed down, contemplated the options, and carefully made his choice: to play outside first. After 5–10 minutes, he returned with his mother, focussed and with a sense of purpose on his face. He then opened up one of the books that he had taken out before, and quietly began reading. While the parents could have made the choice for their son (i.e., told him to sit down and read a book or just taken him outside), there was a very powerful shift in the boy's mindset when the choice was given to him. In fact, he handled the entire situation for all of us, and I believe he felt the gravity and importance of that decision. Though I did, indeed, create the choices, the ultimate decision was entirely his.

If you give your children such choices daily, not only will their decision-making skills improve significantly, but their belief in themselves will also deepen. But, it is a new habit that *you* will have to practise.

You also need to keep in mind that giving choices to your children ultimately helps them to do the things you need them to do. Your children begin to feel that they are being heard and that their needs are being met. Of course, they may negotiate with you now and then, but this is completely all right, as the goal is not just for you to get your way, but for *both* of you to get your ways.

Coaching tip: Avoid giving such choices to children where they don't really have an option and are forced to pick one. All options should be viable and attractive.

Isn't life all about relationships?

The third aspect of teaching your children to believe in themselves is to help them establish strong emotional bonds with family members, friends, and others in society. When children have a positive sense of themselves as well as their social relationships, their capacity to succeed in life rises dramatically. Chief among these relationships is the one between the parents and the child—in which parents should shower their children with love, and do so unconditionally.

A parent recently called me up to tell me how much she loved her son. However, not wanting to spoil him, she asked if there was a limit to how much she should love him.

My reply was, 'There is no limit. You should love him as much as you can.' At the same time, I explained that there are many effective ways of demonstrating that love.

The most primal form of love is expressed through physical means—hugs, kisses, holding hands or similar forms of affection. These gestures have a powerful effect on children's minds. Research shows that children who receive greater amounts of affection in their primary years grow up to be more emotionally secure and stable, and are better able to establish intimate relationships with their own spouses and children.

Appraise your praise

In addition to physical demonstrations of love, parents also express their affection through praise. With each new bit of progress, they eagerly shower their children with compliments such as, 'You sang so beautifully!' or 'Way to go, Tanya, you caught the ball!' or 'Nice job, Manzar, you finished the book.' However, most parents are surprised to learn that extensive praise can actually have a *negative* impact on children.

Sounds surprising? First, when you praise your kids too much, they become focused on just trying to please you and lose interest in the activity itself. Later, if you or others are not around to continuously praise them, they will not be inclined to do that activity. This is true for solving puzzles, doing schoolwork, and even performing social service. They run the risk of becoming addicted to the praise, so much so that in future, they do only what is necessary to get that praise from you—even if that means lying to you!

Second, parents often use praise in an insincere way as a means of distancing themselves. For example, a child tries to show her father a picture she drew while he's reading the newspaper. Without looking up, he says, 'Very good!' While he appears to be praising her, in actuality he is indirectly saying, 'Leave me alone, I'm reading.' False praise is a tactic frequently used by parents who don't want to invest energy in interacting with their children , although it is also done unwittingly by parents who would not do it if they knew better. Either way, whether false praise is uttered by a lazy or an active parent, it has no positive effect on children, as the latter can implicitly sense the insincerity.

Engage with your child

Instead of constantly praising your children, let them know that they are important by being there with them in that moment and interacting with them in a meaningful way. The fact that you engage with them signals clearly to them that they are important, and that you appreciate them even if you don't state it explicitly. In short, it is this togetherness that builds their sense of self-esteem—not merely those casual comments like, 'Great job. Keep it up!' Here are five steps to engage with your children:

1. **Pay attention.** Suppose your child has drawn a picture and wants to show it to you. Stop whatever else you are doing and offer your complete attention. If you are not able to do so, tell him you can't give your attention at the moment, but whenever you are done with what you are doing, you will give him your complete attention.
2. **Make specific observations** about what they are doing. For instance, 'You have drawn a picture of your school ground. I see you drew a school bus as well.' Or, 'I like the way you shaded the bus.'
3. **Ask them questions.** E.g., 'What are these children doing here by the fountain?' Or, 'How do you feel after drawing this?'
4. **Suggest improvements.** E.g., 'It seems as though these lines are not even. Can you make them straighter?'
5. **Make suggestions.** 'Why don't you try drawing the flagpole at your school as well?'

Coaching tip: One way to praise effectively is through 'mirroring', i.e., stating what your child has done. For instance, say things like: 'You were well behaved while I was talking to the doctor', or 'You have climbed the stairs all by yourself!' Doing so, reinforces their good behaviour and encourages them to see themselves as competent individuals.

What matters is your presence not presents

When you spend time with your children, you stimulate the natural opiates in their bodies that cause them to feel good. They, literally, learn to get high from being together with you, and in the process, develop a strong sense of self-esteem.

Interestingly, research tells us that the people who are the happiest in life are not the ones who make the most money but those with the *strongest social bonds*! However, many parents fall prey to the illusion that if they just had a little more money, or a better home, or a new car, or if their kids went to a better school, their lives would be better and they would be happier. In an effort to fulfil this dream, they work harder—six, sometimes seven days a week—and till very late at night. In some families, it is not uncommon that one parent, typically the father, does not return home until after his children have gone to bed, and barely gets to see them at all. He then tries to compensate by buying them gifts. The result: children become insecure due to weak parental bonds, and begin to develop an attachment for material possessions. Therefore, my best advice to parents who are endeavouring exhaustively to give their kids the best they can is this: even if it means taking a slightly lower salary, do so to spend more regular, quality time with your children. You'll enjoy the time with them now, and you'll get a 'pay back' later when your kids turn out to be confident and loving.

Children are little people: they need respect too

I often see parents commanding and yelling at their children as if they were servants, or worse, criminals. 'Get the heck over here right now!' 'I told you to shut up!' 'You're a duffer and you'll never make anything of yourself.' There are also some parents who admit to beating their children well into their teens. When you confront them, they will likely tell you, 'It is for their own benefit.' However, such demeaning treatment will not cultivate a respectful attitude in children any more than a plant will grow by pouring acid on it.

One of the most important things you can do to build your children's belief in themselves is to speak to them and treat them with respect. Respect is something people typically think should be reserved for adults, elders or people with authority. However, sometimes with our loved ones, we let our consideration slip, and speak in a manner that is unbecoming. When parents treat their children disrespectfully, the results can be *extremely* damaging.

It is natural for children to misbehave. It is also natural for parents to lose their patience. However, it's important to note that no matter how frustrated you might feel after the 50th time you've told your kids to switch off the lights when they leave the room, or to play nicely without hitting, you still must treat them with respect. If you label them as naughty, troubled, or problematic, they will begin to believe that that's what they really are. And, if you speak to them sarcastically, insult them, or beat them, they will eventually feel that that is how they are supposed to be treated. Mistreatment will become their norm, and their emotional system will wire itself in a criss-crossed manner that says, 'When people care for me, they abuse me.' The natural extension from this thinking is, 'When I care for someone, I should abuse them.' If you wonder why your children behave disrespectfully towards other kids, their teachers, and even you, try to find out if they are simply aping you. Here are a few ways to inculcate respect in children:

- Use polite language with them, especially when you are unhappy with their behaviour. (E.g., I know you are angry, but hitting is not the right way to express your feelings.)
- Speak to them as mature individuals and not in a 'kiddish' or condescending manner.
- When they don't demonstrate the behaviour that you expect of them, tell them so in a manner that is firm yet respectful. (E.g., 'You are teasing your little brother and that makes him feel very upset. I know you could behave in a much nicer way.')
- Avoid labelling them. (E.g., 'You are lazy.'; 'You are a fool.')

- If you want to teach them something, criticize *the behaviour*, not *the individual*. (E.g., 'Leaving the house without telling me where you are going is not responsible behaviour.')
- Point out their good behaviour when they get it right. (E.g., 'You shared your toys with your cousin and that really made her happy.')

Another aspect of building relationships deals with rules, punishments and rewards. This will be covered in Chapter 6.

Who likes to get labelled?

A young father approached me after a talk I gave for parents on the induction day for new students at a leading school in Amritsar. Eager to get some advice from me about his child who was in Class 1, he inquired, 'Mr Rudolph, I've got a question about my son. How do I get him to write faster? He's so slow that in class he is unable to finish tests and assignments within the given period.' I was getting late for my train back to Delhi, so we walked to the school parking area together while I gave him some suggestions along the way. As we reached the main gate, his son came running over enthusiastically to meet him. 'Here's my son,' he announced. 'The slow writer.' Almost instinctively, the child shrank with embarrassment, as I stood there helplessly watching his self-esteem dissolve into a sense of shame. After offering the boy some words of encouragement, and getting the smile back on his face, I gently pulled the father aside and whispered to him, 'If you keep calling him slow, he'll start believing it.'

Short hand

- By teaching your children to develop a strong sense of self-esteem and a firm belief in their own abilities, you can help them become healthier, happier and able to perform better in whatever they do.

- Help your children identify their dominant Multiple Intelligences and Multiple Natures, as this makes it easy for you to figure out which academic and extra-curricular activities they are more suited to. It can also help you identify the right stream and advise them on the right career path, instead of forcing them to do what they don't like at all.
- It is important to balance praise and criticism in order to help them develop a sense of confidence and self-belief. For creating confidence in children, it is crucial to let them feel special, because when kids know that they have some qualities that make them unique, they develop a positive sense of self-worth that propels them to find meaning and purpose in life.

Law No. 3
Teach your child to explore

Years ago, I was asked to teach English literature at a prominent educational institute. A dedicated teacher, I used to pride myself at my ability to get every student interested in my lessons. However, in one class, there was a girl who was completely indifferent to whatever I did. She was a bit of a rebel, sporting wild clothes, numerous piercings on her face, and a couple of tattoos on her arms and legs. Each period, she sat at the end of the room, her chair propped up on two legs against the wall, chewing gum defiantly with her wide-open mouth, refusing to do any of the assignments I gave. No amount of kindness, scolding or strict action had any effect, and I was at my wit's end about what to do.

One day, in an act of desperation, I walked up to her seat and dropped a stack of twenty white sheets on her desk, and said, 'Listen, I don't care what you write. Just fill up these papers with whatever you want. But, it has to be in English.' A few days later, the girl entered the class and walked straight up to me with a challenging look in her eye, dropping the sheaf of pages on my desk. She then proceeded to her usual place at the back of the class, propped herself up on her chair and folding her arms, started to chew her gum with a look of self-satisfaction. When I picked up the papers, I saw each page was completely filled up with sentences, clippings and colourful drawings—all on her favourite topics: fashion, punk music, body piercing and tattoos. Although her content had nothing to do with the literary topics I was trying to teach, I learnt one valuable lesson: people work hard when they are passionate about the subject matter. And that parents and teachers need to work hard in order to guide their children's interest productively.

According to the Vedas, humans have an in-built drive to 'know'—a natural urge to want to understand the world around them. Unfortunately, adults do not always keep up with a child's insatiable appetite to learn. Parents in nuclear families and urban-based settings have limited time and energy to feed and nurture their child's curiosity. When infants begin to put their hands on everything in sight, moms and dads respond by telling them, 'Don't touch.' When children get older and start asking 'too many questions', they are instructed to 'Keep quiet'. Even in schools, the scenario is not much better; students are packed into factory-style classrooms, are expected to be seen and not heard, and are forced to memorize countless volumes of unrelated information, for the sole purpose of passing exams.

The twenty-odd years of instruction that were supposed to build dynamic human beings, has served more as an obstacle course meant to slow children down. In the majority of cases, children succumb to the suppressive environments both, at home and school. Their impulse to know ends up as a caged animal, which, after years of confinement, loses the wild spark in its eyes. At best, they go on to get 'a job' and lead lives of mediocrity or, as with my rebellious student, manage to buck the system. They avoid the conditioning, but at the same time, wind up becoming confused, alienated, and very often depressed. There is a third, more rare type, however: those who, by some stroke of luck or fate, manage to avoid the shackles, and go on to excel in their lives and achieve their potential.

Coaching tip: The famous scientist Albert Einstein once said, 'I never let my schooling interfere with my education.' So remember: school is not the only place to learn for your children.

However, it is my belief that this third type of individual should be the *norm* rather than the *exception*. In order for that to happen, education (both, at home and in school) must become more than merely an exercise in collecting data—or worse, an activity to keep kids out of our hair while we try to do something else. Education must develop students' interests, opinions, and life skills. It must enable them to cultivate a passion and combine it with their unique abilities. For it is only when they have competence in an area of work, and they are enthusiastic about it as well, will they go on to live life with gusto and achieve something extraordinary.

How can you help your child to explore

Once, a mother of a five year old boy, Rahul, contacted me to seek advice for her son who was extremely outgoing, always experimenting and trying out new things. She was afraid to let him out of her sight because she didn't want him to get hurt.

I told her that it was natural for her to be concerned about her son's safety. However, she would never be able to protect him from every bit of danger that he could possibly confront in life. So, instead of being over-protective, it would be better to allow Rahul the right amount of freedom to explore his world, since children automatically develop a balanced sense of caution.

Mistakes are a part of the game

Making mistakes is part of the learning process. It's plain and simple—if you aren't making mistakes, you aren't learning. Avoid scolding or punishing children for making errors, especially when they are related to exploring their worlds. If your son is trying to do a trick on his bicycle and has a crash, instead of yelling at him for being careless, ask him instead what he was trying to do, how could he have avoided it—and what he learned in the process. If you merely scold him, he'll continue to do crazy things on his bike, but will just hide them from you. (See Chapter 8 for more about making mistakes and Chapter 7 for more on punishment.)

Don't ridicule the ridiculous

In the process of exploring their worlds, children will sometimes wind up saying what seems like the dumbest things. Well, dumb to you because you already have a few decades more of experience in life than they do. You need to recognize their bizarre comments as an attempt of their developing brains to make sense of their world in the best way that they know how, and an opportunity for you to help them clear up their misunderstandings.

When they come out with something amiss, avoid discouraging or insulting them by saying things like, 'What? You don't know that?' or 'That's a silly question.' Such statements can make them feel guilty for their lack of understanding, and could inadvertently erode their self-confidence—even, suppressing their desire to learn. All learning requires some amount of risk-taking, and they should never feel they have to play it safe, thinking, 'I had better not ask questions or I might get scolded for asking something stupid.' If children don't understand something, it means they have not had enough exposure to that concept. Instead of criticizing them, ask them questions about what they have understood so you can identify the knowledge gaps, and provide more accurate perspectives or additional information that will clear up the misconceptions.

> **Coaching tip:** When you find yourself in a position where you do not understand something or do not know the answer to a question, do not hide behind your ego. Admit that you do not know by saying, 'You know, that's a good

question but I don't know the answer.' Then challenge your kids to discover the answer for themselves by asking, 'How could we find out?' In the process, they will learn that not knowing an answer doesn't make you dumb, and that smart people are those who turn a lack of knowledge into an opportunity to learn something new.

Help them make meaning

These days, kids are really smart. They are the ones adults turn to when they need help operating the TV, DVD player, or the computer. Because of their exposure to TV and the Internet, children today are extremely knowledgeable, often knowing more than their teachers and parents about certain subjects. Some parents even feel threatened—and find it hard to retain parental control because they feel their children have outpaced them with their fast and developed minds.

Keep in mind, however, that while your kids might be far ahead of you in certain areas, you are still much more experienced than they are in 'life issues'. Even though they can send an entire three-line text message before you can even find the number 9 key on your cell phone, they still lag far behind you in how to solve social problems and make effective life decisions. Your children desperately need your experience and wisdom to make meaning out of the barrage of information that overloads their minds daily.

Sometimes, parents get stuck when it comes to encouraging their children. They want to push them to their potential, but at the same time, their conscience tells them, 'Hey, they are just kids—let them enjoy their lives. Stop being so strict with them.'

The key to encouraging your children is to make sure they are *challenged*. If kids find the activity too easy, they will quickly lose interest. On the other hand, if the task is too difficult, they may become stressed out and give up.

So, you need to play the role of a facilitator, constantly modifying your children's activities so that they are just above their current ability level.

I'm bored!

This is a phrase that drives many parents crazy. Why do kids lose their interest so quickly, and what can parents do about it? The brain is wired to seek out novelty, which is one reason why the TV is so popular. Kids become bored with their surroundings and various routines, and television provides an endless amount of new content—with pictures, sounds, animation, and so on. However, after a period of time, children can even become bored with the 'same old' stuff on TV. Here are ten tricks to keep your kids entertained:

1. Get them to read story books.
2. Encourage them to cook with you.
3. Provide them with educational board games and puzzles.
4. Let them learn how to play musical instruments.
5. Take them to interesting places (movies, art exhibitions, museums, concerts, the zoo, etc.).
6. Encourage them to do creative writing.
7. Involve them in gardening or taking care of plants.
8. Have them paint, draw and do craft projects.
9. Allow them to participate in after-school activities such as karate, skating, tennis, dance, drama, and so on.
10. Encourage them to observe birds or any animals in nature for an extended time.

Case study

A single mother with two young daughters—Sushmita, aged nine and Namrata, aged eleven—told me that her girls were constantly complaining that they were bored. She shared with me her difficult financial situation—she did not have extra money to buy them a computer or toys, or send them out for after-school activities.

I explained to the woman that it was not a question of money, but a question of applying some ingenuity. There were plenty of activities that would cost her little or nothing, such as gardening, drawing, painting, and writing. They could also borrow books from the library or from friends. It just requires a small amount of effort to decide on the activities and to give your children guidance on how to get started.

What can you do to help your child explore better?

Get them engaged: to their senses

In the days of gurukul, children studied in natural environs, and, as part of their education, were encouraged to commune with nature and learn with all five senses. However, since the age of industrialization, children have slowly been removed from those lush settings, and crammed into environments devoid of greenery. They have lost direct touch with plants and animals, and now learn about them theoretically, through pages in a text book, and vicariously, through their teachers' explanations. Even the so-called 'advanced' instructional systems fail to bridge this gap, inserting one more layer of abstraction between children and their worlds with keyboards and computer screens.

It's not that I am against technology. On the contrary, it's what I am for: holistic education. Researchers tell us that the more our senses are involved in the learning process, and the more we are connected to authentic educational experiences, the more we learn and the longer we retain it. Even though you might not have much control over what goes on at your child's school, you can create more intense instructive experiences for your kids by engaging their senses in learning activities in and around your home. Here are some ways to employ your child's senses:

- Ensure that they spend time outdoors daily in a park or some type of natural surrounding.
- Make sure that they have regular interactions with plants and animals (keeping pets, caring for stray dogs, having an aquarium, gardening, etc.).
- Encourage them to observe everyday objects for longer than usual (birds, insects, people, vehicles, etc.) and to describe, draw or write about them.
- Have them do art work where they use a variety of materials and tools (finger painting, water colours, clay, wood, glass, etc.).
- Let them perform activities that require manipulation of objects (playing with blocks, jigsaw puzzles, Rubik's Cube, etc.).
- Apply aspects from their academic syllabus into real life.

Engage their emotions

Everything we learn first gets filtered through our emotions, and then gets stored in our memories with those emotions attached to them. Emotions colour our learning experiences. So when learners' emotions are positive during the learning process, they tend to absorb more, and store those positive memories with the information and situation they experienced.

One of the most common areas that parents fail to make communicative connections is when their kids come home from school. Most parents ask two standard questions the moment their children are back from school to find out how their kids' day in school was: 'How was school?' or 'What did you learn today?' To which they get the standard replies: 'Fine,' and 'Nothing'. If you have frequently found yourself on the receiving end of such monosyllabic answers, you have only yourself to blame. The reason is your questions failed to stir your children at an emotional level. Consider asking questions about topics that might appeal more to their interest such as their friends, extra-curricular activities they are involved in, important events that are going on, or things that affect them personally and emotionally. Here are some examples of more probing types of questions:

- What was the best part of your day?
- How did you do at today's test?
- What was the funniest part of your day?
- Did you win the football game, debate, or competition (depending upon their interest)?
- How are your friends doing (especially if one of them is unwell)?
- Did anything particularly happy or sad happen?
- If you could redo any part of your day, which would it be and how would you redo it?
- Did you like your lunch today?
- Did you help anyone today?
- What was the most important decision you made today?

You should also give them a chance to ask you similar questions. They will be extremely interested in hearing your own responses, and in turn, will be much more willing to share their own feelings and experiences with you. Try writing 20–30 questions like this on chits of paper and putting them in a box. Whenever your kids come home from school, or whenever you see an opportunity for a few moments of intimate engagement, take turns with them fishing a question or two out of the box. The randomness of which ones turn up will add novelty to the activity, and be fun too.

> **Coaching Tip:** Be careful about when and how you ask your children about their school and friends. Such questions should come naturally while you are serving food, while they are changing, or while serving them meals or bathing them if they are very young. Avoid sounding intrusive or as if you are prying, as your queries might be met with resistance.

Imagine the impossible

Einstein once said, 'Imagination is more important than knowledge'. In attempting to solve some of the most complex problems, he used to imagine himself chasing a beam of light. Hardly the problem-solving tactic a teacher might suggest!

Imagination is the ability to see things in our mind that are not physically present. It might be things that exist in real life, like the holiday destination you visited years ago on a vacation, or the parantha you had yesterday for breakfast. It might also be fantastical things like a crocodile that plays the guitar or a rope so long that you could tie it around the earth. Having a powerful imagination enables children to visualize knowledge—to explore ideas with greater clarity and for longer periods of time; to solve physics problems, to picture what happens inside their bodies when they eat junk food, or to envision solutions to the problem they are currently having with a classmate.

Unfortunately, these days, children's imaginations are weaker than they have ever been, largely due to the increase in watching TV and the decrease in reading books for pleasure. While TV shows and films have the wonderful ability to provide kids with a fully entertaining experience, they leave little to the imagination. Because everything is delivered directly to their senses—visual images, words, sound, music, etc.—they are not challenged to use their imaginations extensively. Below are ten things you can do to fire up your child's imagination:

1. Encourage them to read—especially story books. You should also read to them regularly.
2. Have them tell stories or jokes (insist on plenty of detail).
3. Ask them to close their eyes and minutely describe a person, place, thing—real or make believe.
4. Have them draw something from memory.
5. Get them to try to walk from one location to another blindfolded.
6. Have them describe what their favourite dish tastes like or what it's like to eat it.
7. Have them listen to music with their eyes closed.
8. Encourage them to check out optical illusions in books or websites.
9. Ask them 'what if' questions (e.g., 'What if there were no gravity?', 'What if water cost Rs 200 a litre?', 'What if you had six arms?').
10. Ensure that they spend time with other creative individuals as they will become inspired to explore their imaginations more actively when they see how others do it.

Case study

A father of three children—ages eleven, nine, and five—recently told me about his busy schedule as manager of a major communications company. His busy hours didn't let him spend enough time with his kids, but he was eager to learn about ways in which he could stimulate their minds.

I explained that what was important was that the time he spent with his children be quality time. Even if he didn't get extended blocks of time with them, he could utilize even brief moments together (e.g., when he is driving them somewhere, or waiting in a queue with them) to explore their thoughts, interests, and the world around them. Imagine the impact a single question like this could make in a 30 second elevator ride: 'Did you know that elevators are twenty times safer than escalators?'

Sow the seeds of creativity in your child

British educator, Sir Ken Robinson, defines creativity as 'the process of having original ideas that have value'. A creative bout might involve deciding which object can be used to drive a nail into the wall when a hammer is not available, or even coming up with innovative ways to use the extra crate of mangoes that were gifted by a family friend from Muzaffarnagar.

As adults, we face daily challenges to cultivate novel ways of thinking while exploring solutions to problems. And, as a grateful society, we recognize and reward the value of those who are innovative. Creative people are in great demand in all fields, whether it's business, entertainment, design, education, or journalism. Interestingly, many people believe that when it comes to innovative insight, not all men are created equal. They consider creativity to be something that is doled out in fixed measures at birth—that some folks are, plain and simple, more creative than others. While it is true that we can see differing levels of creativity among people we know, it is a myth that it has fixed limitations that were handed down through the genes.

In short, creativity is something that can be cultivated, and as a parent, you can play a vital role in honing your children's abilities to think innovatively. This, in turn, will empower their capacity to explore, and will significantly contribute to their ability to optimize their potential. This can be done by encouraging them to see the connection between ideas in different ways.

Making connections with schema

Many people think children's minds are like empty vessels that get filled with what they are taught. However, nothing could be further from the truth. Anytime you learn something new, your brain automatically begins searching for old knowledge to connect it with. For instance, if I tell you that a new planet was discovered, and I begin to describe it to you, your brain would automatically pull up previous knowledge of outer space—our sun, the existing planets and so on. This previous knowledge is called 'schema'—kind of like a scaffold or structure that already exists in our minds. As I explain about the new planet, you listen to my description, drawing from your old concept and building upon it, as your brain recreates a fresh model of this new planet and the change to the solar system as you once understood it. Once this fresh model is created in your brain, you now have a new piece of knowledge in your mind that you can further build on.

> **Coaching tip:** Schemas are like starters (appetizers) in a meal. People usually prefer to have a starter in order to get ready for the main course. In the same way, schema can be effectively used like a mental starter before introducing a new idea to a child.

Whenever your children are about to learn something new, you can ready their brains by bringing up the relevant schema. For instance, let's say your son is in primary school, and he is going to study about domestic and wild animals. Instead of just starting him straight into the lesson, ask him the animals he can name, and to tell some of the similarities and differences between them. At this point, the 'animal schema' is fresh in his mind, and his brain is more prepared to make connections and incorporate the new information (that animals can be categorized by their utility to humans) into his conceptual structures. Interestingly, this new information actually gets *physically* connected to the old knowledge. The brain cells associated with each discrete bit of information overlap, much in the same way that a sweater is knitted, with new lines of knitting being hooked on to the previous ones.

> **Coaching tip:** Spend a small amount of time discussing new chapters and topics with your children before they begin. Let them tell you what they already know before jumping into the new chapter.

Compare and contrast

Another way you can help your kids make connections is through compare and contrast—that is, analysing different pieces of knowledge side by side to get a clearer understanding of them. For instance, say your daughter has just learnt about email. You can strengthen her knowledge about email by asking her to compare email and postal mail. She might tell you that both are similar because one is communicating with someone through the written word, and that both can be sent to all parts of the world. She can then contrast the two by saying that postal letters are written on paper, are manually sent and delivered, and take a while to reach their destination while email exists in a digital file, is sent through a computing device, and can arrive at any destination within seconds. Here are five topics on which you can compare and contrast with your children any time:

1. Actors, actresses, famous people
2. Characters in a story

3. Movies and books
4. Places they have visited
5. Things in nature such as animals, plants, and trees

You can even turn the activity into a game, awarding one point for each similarity or difference made.

The Difference Game

Here's a fun game you can play to sharpen your kids' abilities to compare and contrast. Ask them what's the difference between a _________ and a _________. You can fill in the answers randomly or by drawing them out of a hat. See who can come up with the funniest answers.

Example: What's the difference between a cup of tea and a brick?

Answer: A cup of tea keeps a person up and a brick keeps a building up. Variations you can play are: **What do these have in common?**

'What do _________ and _________ have in common?'

Example: What do milk and cell phones have in common? **Answer:** If you drop them on the floor, there's going to be trouble.

What do you get? 'What do you get when you cross a _________ and a _________?'

Example: What do you get when you cross a rickshaw driver and a toothbrush?

Answer: Someone who'll brush your teeth for five rupees, but who will make you share the brush with someone else.

Putting the pieces together

I am sure everyone has heard about the story of the three blind men and an elephant. Each person feels the animal and describes it to the others. The one feeling the leg says, 'It's like a tree.' The one feeling the tail says, 'It's like a rope.' And the one feeling the ears says, 'It's like a big blanket.' Similarly, children often learn bits and pieces of information, but fail to tie them together and see how they fit together meaningfully.

So, whenever your child is learning something, help her see the bigger picture. What is the underlying principle behind it? For instance, if your child is learning about the Revolt of 1857, help him understand that this is an issue about Freedom and Power. Helping children see the 'bigger idea' provides meaning in their lives, enabling them to understand not just 'what' is going on in the world, but also how and why.

Once your children learn to make connections between things, take them a step further and help them make 'deep connections' between things that are related, though they may not explicitly appear to be so. For example, have them:

- Compare a cell and a factory
- Link an ice cream seller's sales with the change of weather
- Identify Newton's Laws of Motion in stunts performed by an actor in a film
- Explain why there are more or fewer power cuts at a particular time of year
- Explain how a politician's decision to tie up with another party would give him a power advantage

What is Higher Order Thinking Skills (HOTS)?

Questions can be incredible tools for learning—as mighty as atom bombs. However, most parents and teachers ask questions that are weaker than a water pistol. Asking questions only for gathering information such as, 'What is the symbol for the chemical sodium?' or 'What score did you get on your test?' does little to stimulate children's thinking.

Their brains need bigger challenges to grow and to become powerful. Parents need to learn how to ask questions that will really put their children's grey matter to the test. The solution here lies in asking questions that kindle their Higher Order Thinking Skills (also referred to as HOTS). HOTS are the mental muscles that we use when we have to make decisions, solve problems, analyse things, come up with new ideas, make judgements, form opinions, and so on. In short, they are used in every sphere of life throughout our lives.

You can ask these HOTS questions to your kids to keep their minds sharp—at home, while travelling, and anywhere else that you spend time with them. Below are examples of HOTS questions related to a variety of topics:

Academics

- Can you think of another way to solve this maths problem?
- Which lesson is your favourite so far in civics?
- What does swaraj mean to you in your own words?

Family and relationships

- What do you think life was like when your grandmother was your age?
- Aditya seems upset. How can you tell?
- If Gautam Uncle had his very own theme song, what would it be?

Schedules

- Why is it important to have a schedule?
- How could you change your schedule to make it more effective?
- If no one kept a schedule, what would the world be like?

Around the home

- How can we prevent the milk from spilling in the refrigerator?
- What is an inexpensive way in which we can make our home more beautiful?
- What should we do tonight instead of watching TV?

While shopping

- Why do you think those shawls are so expensive?
- When are oranges available in the market?
- Other than this route, how else could we get to the bazaar?

Fun times

- Do you like this painting? Why or why not?
- Which animal are you most similar to?
- What does that cloud shape look like to you?

Coaching tip: To create meaningful HOTS questions, try using all kinds of interrogative words such as: who, what, where, when, why, how. Also, add other words like can, could, should, and might (e.g., Who could...?, What might...?).

Whenever you interact with your kids, ask yourself if your questions are challenging their higher thinking or not. If not, try to make your queries more thought provoking. Asking HOTS questions gives your kids' minds a complete workout, and unlocks their potential to learn more comprehensively, helping them become better problem solvers. Ever since the CBSE introduced HOTS questions in its examinations in 2008, there is a compelling academic reason why your kids should be exploring concepts in greater depth.

Get them thinking out of the box

Too often, people get into routines and habits, and their perception of things around them begins to dull. Another way of getting your children to keep their spirit of exploration alive is to encourage them to think differently about their day-to-day world. Here are five things you can encourage them to do:

1. **Try new types of food:** Have your kids try new foods and cuisines to tickle their taste buds in innovative ways. This opens doors to learning about different cultures and languages as well.
2. **Visit new places:** Whether it's a foreign country or just an unexplored part of your neighbourhood, exciting new worlds are waiting to be discovered.
3. **Try doing the same things differently:** Ask them to try brushing their teeth with their other hand, take a different route to school, or put on their tie with their eyes closed.
4. **Go beyond the textbooks:** Explore the subjects that your children have learnt in school through movies, TV, the Internet, biographies, and so on, and help them stay steps ahead of textbooks.
5. **Get familiar with the unfamiliar:** Challenge your kids to learn about unfamiliar topics—especially things that are way outside their syllabus—such as musical instruments of tribal Africans or quarks.

Coaching tip: Don't just let your kids have all the fun in the throes of exploration. Join in alongside them to become their knowledge discovery partner. Not only will it benefit your kids, it will also stimulate your own neural networks and rekindle your own love of learning.

Short hand:

- Children have an innate drive to learn. As a parent, it is your responsibility to create an environment that enables that drive to flourish.
- Encourage your children to find a purpose in what they do, to connect concepts to find meaning, and to ask questions to uncover answers to their curiosity.
- Teach them to venture out courageously into the unknown, and stay close by on their journey so that you can help them make sense of things along the way.
- You can easily guide children in organizing and remembering what they have learnt by means of smart tools such as schemas, compare-and-contrast, and spot-the-difference.
- Make room for mistakes that your children are sure to commit on the path of exploring and learning, and get involved in the process of investigating alongside them.

Law No. 4
Teach your children to make goals

One evening, I was at a friend's house. Anita, his eleven year old daughter, had just finished her final exams and was lazing about watching TV, while my friend and I talked. My friend made a comment about his daughter's tendency to watch TV all the time, so I took it as an opportunity to put my method into practice. I sat down on the couch next to Anita and asked her what she had planned for the next two weeks during her vacation. She looked at me in a most puzzled manner and said, 'Um, nothing really. My school work is done, so my plan is to do nothing but watch TV for the next two weeks.' I then told her that she had a perfect opportunity to cultivate her hobbies, and learn new things in this extra time. She was amused and baffled at the same time, and laughed in protest, 'But I don't have any goals!' To which I replied, 'That's an even *better* reason to write them down! But, first, we have to make some.'

She shut off the TV, shuffled into her bedroom with a sense of compliance, and returned with a copy and a pen. However, her reluctance began to give way after a few explanations and some gentle prodding. She then began to list out a few areas she wanted to work on: improving mathematics, learning to sketch, getting better at dance. Then others started to flow: learning to make bracelets, learning to prepare food, and even a secret desire to learn Spanish. Within no time, her list grew to about twelve goals and her eyes grew wide with them. Though the items had been roughly jotted down at first, we spent another 10 minutes making them more specific and time-bound. Within 25 minutes, she was armed with a list of powerful goals—her own goals—and she looked at them with a sort of amazement, and with a sense of pride and ownership of them, as if suddenly she had a new set of friends—a new purpose to live for.

What are goals?

Goals are objectives that people create in order to give themselves a sense of purpose in life. When one has goals, one has a direction to move in—a way to focus one's energy to get things accomplished, and then derive a sense of satisfaction in one's abilities and efforts. It is not incorrect to say that without goals, one would accomplish little, or at least, not in the way one would want.

Like adults, children, too, need goals to help them concentrate and stay focused during the course of their childhood. Below are the different types of goals that children can set for themselves:

Academic Goals

a. Getting at least 5th position in my class by the end of this year.
b. Getting an aggregate of at least 85 percent this term in my science exams.

Extra-Curricular Goals

a. Doing a solo dance performance in front of an audience on Diwali.
b. Creating my own blog/website with my own poems within six weeks.

Personal Goals

a. Losing five kilos of weight in the next five months.
b. Controlling myself from hitting my little sister when I am angry at her.

Social Goals

a. Plant at least ten trees in this year.
b. Teach an illiterate child how to read the alphabet by the end of the school holidays.

Family Goals

a. Calling my grandparents at least once a week for 10 minutes.
b. Making a scrap-book of our family photo album for mom and dad's wedding anniversary.

Have a goal planning meeting

Now that you have an idea about the different types of goals, it's time to get down to business and get your children to make some of their own. However, don't be surprised if they just don't automatically start making their own lists of goals. You will need to play an important role as a coach to get them into action, and to guide them through the process.

To begin with, choose a day when you have plenty of time, when there is no other pressing work to be done, and when your kids are in the right mood (if exams are right around the corner, or if their favourite TV show is on, you might find it extremely hard to get their attention).

Sit down with them, ask them what they think goals are, and why everyone should have them. It's helpful if you share the goals in your own life with your children, as they will learn best with examples. Then tell them how important it is for them to have goals in their lives as well.

Brainstorm with your kids to help them create goals for themselves. If they are confused about which type of goals to create, spend a little time talking about their interests and passions. Find out if they have any dreams or aspirations—things they would like to achieve in the coming year—or at any point in their lives. Your kids might only pick a few categories to begin with, such as academic goals and personal goals—and that's fine. If this is new to them, first let them get used to it.

Don't force them to make goals or try to set their goals yourself. Instead, play an active role as a coach, listening closely to what they have to say and asking them critical questions to probe their thinking: 'Why do you want to choose that goal? Is there another goal that might be more suitable?'...and so on. In doing so, you will lead them to establish goals that are appropriate, that they are happy with, and that they feel ownership of. You don't want your children to feel that the brainstorming session was merely an exercise for you to control them, and make them do everything you want, whether they like it or not!

It is up to you to gauge your children's abilities, and help them set reasonable goals accordingly. Find a balance between having too many (which might overwhelm them) and too few (which might make them feel underchallenged).

Coaching tip: There's nothing like having a great role model. Be sure to make a personal set of goals for yourself. Watching you set your own goals, your kids will get excited and become more inspired to do the same for themselves.

Writing down your goals does work!

After your kids have chosen their goals, it's time for them to start writing them down. You can have them use the SMART model to ensure the goals are clear, appropriate and effective. The SMART method suggests that when you make a goal, you ensure that each one is:

1. **Specific:** Your children should be able to clearly articulate their goals.

☹ to do well in science.
☺ to get aggregate of at least 85 percent this term in my science classes this year.

2. **Measurable:** They should be able to measure their goals in quantity or quality.
   ☹ to plant trees in our neighbourhood.
   ☺ to plant at least ten trees in our neighbourhood.
3. **Accurate:*** They should be according to the nature and interest of the child.
   Example: for a child with strong Linguistic Intelligence and weak Mathematical Intelligence
   ☹ to finish a 150-page book of maths challenges over the summer holidays.
   ☺ to keep a diary, writing one page everyday on topics of 'my interest' over the summer holidays.
4. **Realistic:** They should be according to the ability of the child.
   Example: for a child who is struggling in maths with 40 percent marks.
   ☹ to get 95 percent marks on his final report in maths.
   ☺ to get 55 percent marks on his final report card in maths.
5. **Time bound:** Fix a time frame for the goals to be accomplished.
   ☹ to give up eating meat.
   ☺ to completely give up meat within three months.

* Although others refer to this item as 'Attainable', I prefer to use 'Accurate' instead.

Below are five tips to make your goals-setting session a success:

1. Don't hijack the session

Resist the temptation of making all the decisions regarding your children's goals yourself.

2. Getting your points in

After your children have had the chance to identify a few of their goals, share some of your concerns about them—things that you would like to see them improve, such as getting specified marks in certain subjects, or improving their table manners. Try to arrive at a balance that makes both of you comfortable.

3. Handling objections

If your children object to any of the items you put on the list, discuss it with them. Ask them what their reasons are, and decide whether or not you can negotiate with them. Where you are willing to negotiate, give them choices, and make trade-offs. For instance, if you want them to clean the dishes every night, but they object because there is a TV show they want to watch right after dinner, you can get them to agree to watching the TV show and then cleaning the dishes afterwards. Or, if you want to see them wake up at 5:30 am so they can be on time for the bus, but they feel it's too early, perhaps you can agree to their waking up at 5:45 am.

4. Remember that each child is different

As you work with your children to establish their goals, keep in mind that all children are different, and that their individual goals will not end up being same—even if they are twins! Avoid making identical or very similar goals for your kids, and instead, ensure that the goals they come up with are genuinely tailored to their unique personalities, interests, and aspirations.

5. Keep it fun

Make the goal-setting exercise enjoyable—don't get too heavy about the entire affair, but keep a light-hearted attitude about the process. For instance, if you want them to keep their rooms tidy or fold laundry, see if you can turn the goal into a race or competition.

Once this is done, have them make a goals chart that they can put on their bedroom wall. They can create the chart on colourful paper and decorate it the way they like. Seeing their goals again and again will constantly remind them of the targets they need to stay focused on.

Watch over your kids

While there are some children who are very independent in chasing their goals and need little follow up, most require regular supervision. Do not think that if they slack off, there is something wrong with them—it is natural for kids to get distracted easily. Keeping them on task is the foremost job of a parent—a job that requires continuous feedback and support throughout the entire year.

Note that the number of times, and the length of time, you will need to check in with your kids will vary from child to child—it could be anywhere from everyday to a few times a week or from a few minutes to half hour or more. Whatever the case may be, the rule of thumb is to keep your interaction regular.

Case study

Last year, a parent from my school came into my office with his ten year old son, Arjun, complaining about his performance and behaviour. He began by blaming Arjun's teachers, and then started speaking critically of his son, saying how lazy and irresponsible he was. When he had finished, a few questions from my side determined that a) the boy had no clear goals, and b) there was no one who was monitoring him at home at all. His wife did not make any effort to look into her son's activities, and he himself used to come home late daily and would also not make any effort.

I eventually convinced him to create a set of goals, tailor-made for Arjun, and to spend just 15 minutes with him everyday. Within two weeks, the man returned, expressing his gratitude, as not only Arjun's performance had begun to shoot up, his behaviour problems had also disappeared—all with an investment of just 15 minutes per day.

You can use different techniques to bring your child back on track. When you see your children going off course, don't immediately start scolding them. First, try to identify the root cause of the problem, and then pick the strategy that will work best to get them back in line. (See Rules, Chapter 6, page 84 for more on this). Perhaps, the goals might not be clear enough, or maybe they are too difficult. Or, maybe they just need a bit of prodding. Here are a few strategies you can adopt to ensure your child remains focused and motivated:

- Take interest to discuss their goals with them. Note the achievements they have already made. Then remind them of their goals, and why they are trying to achieve them.
- Join them in any goal-related activity for a short while, and demonstrate how enjoyable it can be.
- Go back to the SMART model to see if the goals are not appropriate in some way. Then, revise them or let your children modify/change their goals if they are really not working.
- Remind them of famous people who overcame great odds in achieving their goals.

- Let them know how much you love them, and that you are there for them whenever they need help.
- If nothing seems to be working, consider limiting other activities that they want to do until they complete the ones they should.

Challenges keep the goals alive

So many parents ask me how they can motivate their kids, especially when they fail to succeed with all types of rewards and punishments. Actually, the best way to ignite the fire within your kids is to give them goals that are appropriate—ones that genuinely match their interests and abilities. Armed with such goals, children have the most important thing in the world: *challenge*—situations that test their minds and bodies—which dare them to see if they can accomplish the task by themselves. Challenges appeal greatly to children's sense of autonomy and competence, and motivate them internally, removing the need of external incentives like toys, money (or a slap!). Further, when kids manage to conquer a goal by themselves, they become inspired to seek out the next one—and the virtuous cycle continues.

Short hand

- Goals begin with dreams, but then they need to be carefully defined to fit your children's natures, interests and abilities.
- As a life coach, you need to remain closely involved to monitor your kids' progress, checking in with them regularly to ensure their goals are well adjusted, and that they get regular doses of inspiration from you.
- By creating the right type of challenges for your kids, you ensure that they will remain motivated, and will move on a path towards independently setting and chasing their own goals in future as well.

Law No. 5
Teach your children to plan

A businessman from New Delhi approached me last year because his nineteen year old son, Gaurav, had, according to him, this 'crazy idea' of wanting to be a professional basketball player in the United States. His son was obsessed with his goal and would not listen to a word his father said about the matter—especially his suggestions about joining the family business. Though enrolled in an expensive private college, he had all but dropped out of the institution, spending time there only to use its sports facilities.

When I met the son, I was impressed with the passion with which he spoke about his aim in life. However, after I asked a few questions about the specific, step-by-step route to his destination, he began to falter, and it was apparent that he had not really thought out his plan clearly. I then took a huge piece of chart paper and asked him to draw me a road map from where he was now, to a point in time where he could qualify as a professional American basketball player. As he did so, it became even more evident that he was already lagging, and that if he wanted to achieve his dream, it wasn't enough for him just to practise by himself. He would need the experience of actually playing on a team, which he could only get from a college. And to continue there, he would need to attend classes as well.

In addition, there were doubts to consider as well: What if he didn't pass his classes? What if he made it to a US university but didn't make the college team? And ultimately, what if, after all that work, he did not get drafted into the pros? After an hour of rigorous discussion, we emerged with a detailed plan that mapped out his route to playing professional basketball—as well as alternative plans that included becoming a sports coach, the owner of a sporting goods store, an outdoor adventure guide, and if all else did not go as planned, a partner in his father's business. Both, he and his father, were completely satisfied. As they were leaving, the son said to me, 'Why didn't they teach us this in school? Every kid in India should have to go through this process.'

If your kids want to make their dreams become a reality, they need to learn how to create practical plans. This is essential to execute their goals. They must be able to see a route or direction to follow that will give them the confidence to reach their desired destination. The art of planning begins with goals—which we talked about in the previous chapter. However, to achieve these goals, you need to help your child plan in breaking them down into smaller, achievable objectives. For instance, let's say your son sets a goal of 'doing really well in maths'. To achieve this larger goal, you need to create smaller, more manageable goals that lead to the realization of this dream, such as 'I will get a final grade of at least 80 percent marks in maths this year', or 'I will get at least 82 percent on my next maths unit test'.

Make a timetable

Having a routine or timetable is one of the key factors to becoming disciplined—especially for children. By following a definite routine, they will become more effective and efficient at whatever they are pursuing—academic achievement, extra-curricular activities, hobbies, etc. However, as you have likely experienced, getting children into fixed patterns of behaviour can be a big challenge. They vehemently resist the structuring of their time, as for the first few years of their existence, life was organized entirely around their own needs and desires—and they became used to that. So, when parents complain to me that their kids don't follow a routine or waste a lot of time, I wonder why they are so surprised. What makes them think that their children will willingly start imposing restrictions on themselves?

When parents complain about children having a time-management problem, initial investigations usually reveal that the children follow no fixed timetable. And if they do, it was one that was made a long time ago, and is buried in a copy somewhere. That's why I recommend that parents work with their children to make clear routines. And, here I emphasize the word *with*. You should not make the routines *for* them—your children must play a central role in creating the timetables with their own hands, as it will foster a sense of ownership in them. And, as a role model for your child, you should set the standards yourself.

Case study

Not too long ago, a mother and father came to me with their son, Abhishek, who was in Class 2. They were full of complaints about his sleeping late, dilly-dallying in the morning, and constantly being late for school. I explained to them the importance of creating a morning routine for him, and suggested they begin with the father showing their son a written plan of his own morning routine. The man looked at me blankly, and stated, 'You know what, I don't even have a morning routine.' After this came the realization, 'So you mean, I have to make my morning routine, too?' With a smile, I told him, 'Yes, exactly!' He realized the importance of setting an example as a role model with his own routine.

Ensure your children have regular routines for:

- Morning—from the time they wake up until the time they go to school.
- After school—from the time they get home from school till the time they are ready to go to bed.
- Evening—from the time they complete their homework, eat/etc., until the time they sleep.

By and large, your children's morning and evening routines should remain consistent. The after-school routine may change depending upon the time of year and what is happening at that particular time (the beginning of the school year, exam time, etc.). Everybody needs a break—even your children—so try to set different routines for weekends, holidays, summer vacation, etc. Ensure routines are posted in a location that is easy for your children to see (e.g., their bedroom wall), because if it is just tucked away in their desk drawer, it is likely to be ignored. Lastly, there must be accountability. Keep checking in with your children on their routines to make sure they are following them. A small bit of follow up goes a long way in keeping them moving in a disciplined manner.

> **Coaching tip:** If you feel your own planning abilities are not very strong, involve your spouse or another adult who is more adept at it. Different parents have different strengths in their skill sets, and can work as great partners in coaching.

At the same time, do not pick up all the slack. There is also the case of some parents who are excellent planners, but who hamper their children's learning skills by assuming all the planning responsibilities themselves. Their children then become dependent on them, and as a result, wind up being lazy and don't develop their own sense of planning. Ensure you pass on these organizing skills by *involving them* in the planning process. Come up with plausible options and give them choices. For example: 'From 4:00 pm to 5:00 pm you can either play outside or do some reading for pleasure. Which would you prefer?'

Once your children get comfortable with following routines, it's time to sharpen their time-management skills further. Here are a number of strategies you can follow to help your children make the best use of their time.

Make to-do lists

Maintaining a to-do list is a very powerful habit to develop. Fewer things slip out of the mind, and it keeps a check on procrastination. My father taught me how to keep a to-do list when I was in school. A lawyer, with so many clients, cases, and tasks to maintain, he showed me his own list that ran down the entire length of a legal page. I became inspired by his example, and immediately started making my own. One day, bursting with pride, I remember telling him, 'Dad, I have eighteen things on my to-do list!' To which he replied, 'You should always have things on your to-do list. Because when your list is finished, life is finished.' Since then, I've continuously maintained to-do lists that contain dozens of items, and which I feel has accounted for my efficiency in work.

You can have your children keep a to-do list. They can keep their list in a diary or a small book. Get them in the habit of reviewing the list in the morning, as well as at the end of the day. If they have completed any items on their list, have them cross those items off. Then see if you can encourage them to add new items.

Coaching tip: Tips offered only through spoken words run the risk of disappearing into thin air. Improve the chances of your advice being followed by delivering it in written form as well (e.g., personalized letters, lists of important suggestions and post-it notes stuck in a visible place).

Make prioritization a priority

Prioritization is the art of organizing tasks in the order of their importance. It is a good start for your children to have their to-do lists, but if they only do the things they enjoy or the things that are easiest, they will likely find themselves in a difficult situation down the line where they have not completed an important piece of work on time. When teaching your children to prioritize, do the following:

- Have them make their to-do list.
- Ask them to rate/rank the items by labelling them important (I), very important (VI), and less important (LI) (or any other system that makes sense to them).
- Then have them re-write the list with the VIs first, the Is second, and the LIs last.

Have them refer again and again to their list to cross off items, add new items, and re-prioritize. Keep in mind, as with your own life, sometimes priorities change. Sometimes, teachers change their plans and routines, exams are postponed, and so on.

Lastly, it is important to know that prioritization has wide reaching implications for children, such as for getting homework completed on time, being prepared for examinations, and effectively taking exams. It is a skill which, once developed, will benefit your children in all areas of their lives and learning.

Respecting deadlines

An important part of planning and accomplishing things is having clear, plausible deadlines—and a respect for them as well. Whenever an important piece of work is given to your children, be it a school assignment or a home responsibility, ensure that they remain aware of the due dates.

How can you help? First, have them keep a wall calendar, where they can write the dates down. Second, regularly review their calendars with them and remind them of the upcoming deadlines. Frequent, gentle reminders *to get started early* will help them avoid waiting till the last moment to complete their work. This will enable them to sufficiently immerse themselves in their work so that they are able to enjoy the learning process. When they are short of time, there's no opportunity to get blissfully lost in one's work—the shortage of time creates pressure, and stress, which don't permit that state of work or learning. At that point, there's no time—they just have to hurry up and get it done. In the process, they might even realize that, 'Hey, this is actually pretty interesting,' but then not be able to enjoy it. What a shame.

When I tell parents to ensure their kids have schedules, many rush out and make the schedules for their children immediately. However, they are disappointed when their kids totally ignore them.

There's a good reason for this. If you make the schedule yourself, your kids won't feel ownership for it. Whenever you make the schedule, do it together with your children. If they are old enough to write, it's better that you have them write it down in their own hand. Then, when they are not going as per the plan, you only need to remind them that they are not following *their* schedule. Chances are that they will be much more inclined to follow it.

Balancing work and play

Sometimes children receive so many school assignments, tests, and other learning responsibilities that they become overwhelmed. You know how it feels—when you have so many things to do, and you don't even know where to begin. In such cases, children often become so anxious due to the mental overload that their brain literally shuts down. They then handle the situation in one of the only ways they know how: avoidance. They will watch TV, surf the net, play video games, eat, read comics, talk on the phone with their friends—anything else but work.

As the saying goes, 'All work and no play makes Jack a dull boy'. Play is an essential part of our lives—whether it's playing sports, games, or getting into some kind of entertainment. Studying more and more will not yield better results. In fact, a person who studies a little less and adds some play into his routine will, in the long run, wind up having less stress, scoring better on tests and being happier, in general, in life. (You will read more about the benefits of Play in Chapter 7.)

It might sound counter-intuitive, but excessive studying is *not* beneficial for learning. In fact, excessive studying results in stress, which leads to less efficient learning. So, when you work with your children to create their routines, ensure they have sufficient time set aside for play. At the same time, you need to keep in mind that *all* play and no work certainly won't make Jack a sharp boy. Use your discretion and make sure there is adequate time set aside for both.

So, what can you do as a parent to help your child lead a balanced life? Keep your eyes open to detect when your children are reaching a saturation point. Explain to them that when they feel unable to manage their work by themselves, it's perfectly okay to seek help—to find someone who can assist them in getting organized. Have them use their Self-O-Meter to detect when they feel overloaded (refer to page 22), and when they do, to identify someone (you, a grandparent, an older sibling, etc.) who can help them get back on track, especially with respect to scheduling and prioritizing tasks.

On weekends, especially Sundays, children have a lot of time on their hands. So, keep a special routine for weekends, though I suggest you change the routine around a bit. Give your children a strong say in their plan as well. Just watch—they will be amazed at how much they can accomplish in a single day when they regulate their times.

Case study

A few years ago, a father sent me an email about his son, Prashant, who was studying at an IIT. Although Prashant was extremely studious and well organized, his health was poor, as he complained of a lack of appetite and weak eyesight. And while he was scoring well on exams, he was reclusive and his mood seemed very dark.

I explained to him how important it was to balance out Prashant's schedule. Merely having a schedule and following it will not yield complete success. A schedule has to be balanced in the same way that a diet must be balanced. There should be a variety of activities—not just studying day and night. His father spoke with him and convinced him to set aside two hours daily for exercizing and socializing. He agreed and began playing an hour of table tennis followed by an hour of playing guitar with his friends. As a result, his son's mood lifted and his appetite increased. Even with studying two hours less, his results did not drop—but the quality of his life improved significantly.

Multitasking can be too taxing

In our fast-paced world, we are sometimes inclined to do more than one thing at a time in order to do all of the things we wish to do. This is referred to as multitasking. We often see children trying to double up their efforts by watching TV and simultaneously doing homework, or having a conversation while reading—and switching back and forth between the two. While some people pride themselves at being great multitaskers, it is a practice that I frown down upon.

I believe any task deserves full and undivided attention. While multitasking, each activity gets half of your attention, and you do neither particularly well. It also puts you at risk of making mistakes. So, if you notice your children talking on the phone while practising their maths, stop them and get them to segment their time. Tell them to finish their call and then work, or vice versa. This will enable them to apply their complete concentration to each task, so they can do each task with a greater degree of success.

I am surprised by how many parents permit their kids to do their homework with the TV on. Neither are the kids able to concentrate on what they are studying nor are they able to enjoy the TV shows.

Teach your kids that when it's time to work, they should just work. Likewise, when it's time to enjoy, only enjoy. Whatever they are doing, they should give that particular activity their undivided attention. If you see them trying to do their homework with the TV on, give them the option of either doing their homework first and watching TV, or watching their show and then finishing their homework.

Help your children to assess themselves

From time to time, talk and discuss with your children about their development. Have them review their particular goals to gauge what progress they are making. While children are very much used to being assessed by others, such as parents and teachers, they are not always explicitly aware of their feelings about their own growth. As such, self-assessment is a powerful practice that they should learn to engage in.

For instance, let your children rate themselves on how well they think they have been following their daily routines, performing in their studies, helping around the house, etc. I suggest you make a simple rating system, like a 5-point scale (where 5 is the highest and 1 is the lowest). I don't think it is vital for you to rate your children. Instead, give them the option of rating themselves.

> **Coaching tip:** Get your children to rate you too! And why not? They might give you some suggestions on how you could make some improvements as well!

Make review meetings and self-assessment a regular affair (e.g., weekly, fortnightly, or monthly) and do it informally, as a matter of course. Although, frequency is important, consistency is more essential. Ensure your meeting is not skipped, and be certain to give sufficient time, concentration, and consideration to your children during the meeting.

Get them involved

Don't just do all the planning yourself for holidays, family events and festivals. Instead, involve your children. For instance, if your child's birthday is coming up, let him or her be involved in the planning process. How would he or she like to celebrate it? Where will it be held? Who will be invited? Will there be invitation cards? What will they say? What activities will the children do? Which food items will be served? And what about return gifts?

Try this for any type of events such as anniversaries, weddings, etc. Even if some things might be beyond their abilities, you can still have them sit with you while you engage in the planning process and ask them for inputs.

This helps them to extend their planning skills and makes them feel responsible at the same time. Inadvertently, you would have instilled valuable life skills that would stand them in good stead throughout their lives.

Make a family plan!

Suppose you are planning a trip to a relative's house, or maybe a family vacation. If so, it is a perfect opportunity to engage your children in such decisions:

- Where will you go?
- For how many days?
- What will you do each day?
- How will you travel there?
- What will you need to carry with you?
- Which games, toys, puzzles, books, etc., should you pack to keep you busy during downtimes?
- Should you take any music along (if in car, on train, etc.)?

Keep a home calendar

Keep a home calendar that contains different events on it. Of course, have your children participate actively in the process. The calendar can contain holidays, test dates, vacations, and so on. When new items come up, have your children add them to the calendar. Maintaining a home calendar involves your children in a genuine planning process that adds to their scheduling skills.

Short hand

- Coach your children on how to create practical plans in order to help them execute their goals and make their dreams become a reality.
- The first step towards educational planning is to create definite, practical routines— in consultation

with your kids—to help them see a route or direction to follow in order to reach their desired destination.

- The other important thing, after having prepared the routines, is to follow-up with their compliance, which becomes easier if you make and follow your own routines, and be a role model for your children.
- The efficiency of whatever your children are pursuing—academic achievement, extra-curricular activities, hobbies, etc.—increases with a little fine tuning of their routines. This includes making to-do lists, using prioritization techniques, and respecting deadlines.
- Teaching your children to assess themselves and involving them in family planning are some of the best ways to turn them from being passive observers into active go-getters.

Law No. 6
Teach your children the rules of the game

Not long ago, I was invited for dinner at the home of a couple in Noida. Before entering their first floor home, I could hear the squeals of children at play, a sound not unfamiliar in urban, nuclear family settings in India. As I entered, the grand marble exteriors of the house's façade promised to reveal a beautiful, well maintained home. However, my eyes bulged out with surprise when the door opened: pillows and cushions were thrown helter-skelter, toys and notebooks littered the floor, and painted cement walls were heavily marred with crayon.

My hosts seemed blind to the chaotic state of their home, as if there was a white elephant in the room and no one seemed to notice. When their two boys charged into the room, chasing each other with plastic guns and screaming at the top of their voices, I cringed.

During our conversation, my attention was diverted by the two boys aged five and seven , who oscillated between watching cartoons, to play fighting, and back to their art work on the walls. When it was time for dinner, their mother threatened to turn off the TV if they did not eat. Her threat, however, proved futile as minutes after she returned to the kitchen, the boys were off, chasing each other again with their guns a'blazing.

When we had finished eating, the mother made a reference to her naughty boys and her constant frustration with them—their hyperactivity, aggressive behaviour, disrespectful manner of speaking, and so on. 'You're an educator,' she said. 'What can we do?' she asked. I shed the niceties, and exposed the truth to them: the problem was not the boys, but the husband and wife, who failed to implement any rules in their home. I also told them that if they didn't do something about it soon, it would get worse.

Who makes these rules and why do we need them anyway?

The first place we need to start is by looking at the rules in your own home. Do you have rules in your own home? Which ones? Are they clear to you and your kids? One of the most important things about being successful with rules, is ensuring they are explicit—that they are not just made up on the spot according to your own moods. Rather, that they are fixed, properly explained, and even put in writing, so they are truly in black and white. When rules are not expressly clarified, children often get confused by their parents' seemingly inconsistent reactions to their behaviour. For example, one day they watch TV for four hours and you say nothing to them about it. The next day, they watch for three hours and you yell at them for watching too much TV. And the day after that, you seem to have no problem with it when they again have a marathon viewing session of five hours.

Rules can only be effective when they are made known to all parties involved. Therefore, the best place for you to begin is by having a rule-making session.

When there are rules, and people follow them, there is order. And having order makes life better, as it helps us achieve our goals more easily. Take the road for instance. When people follow the traffic rules, it makes it easy for all drivers to navigate their cars and reach their destinations safely. However, when people don't follow rules, it makes driving a frightening, and even dangerous, experience.

How to go about making your own rules?

Pick a time to meet with your kids when there is no time constraint. Set aside 30–60 minutes to explain to them that in order to maintain discipline in the home, and to create an environment where members can get along well, you would like to make a set of rules. You can call it 'the family rules' or 'the Gupta household constitution', or whatever else you would like to refer to it as.

Begin by identifying a number of categories under which your rules will fall, such as:

- Daily routines
- Cleanliness
- Food and eating
- Household duties
- Homework
- TV

You might wish to identify particular problems that you have been having with your kids, and to ask them to create rules regarding each of them. For instance, your kids often eat while watching TV or don't finish all the food on their plate. You can make rules such as:

- We may not watch TV while we eat.
- We should only take on our plate what we can finish eating, and should not waste any food.

When it comes to the actual writing of the rules, I would suggest that rather than you penning them down, let your kids do it, as when they write them down with their own hands, it will give them a sense of ownership.

After a rough draft of the proposed rules has been drawn up, they can then be written on a fair page, a set of pages, or on a chart. You can let your kids decorate them as well, and keep them in a place that's easy to see or locate so you can consult them whenever you require. Be sure to review the rules from time to time, and be prepared to amend them where required. Rules should not exist for the rules' sake, but for the sake of enabling your family to get along peacefully.

> **Coaching tip:** Make sure that children know there are often different rules for adults and children. However, be sure you set an example and follow the rules you expect your kids to follow.

Rules around the home

While there are rules of all sorts that you and your kids can think of, there are two topics regarding which parents frequently ask me questions: watching TV and pocket money. Below are suggestions about how you can address both areas with a high degree of success.

TV: how much is not too much?

In many ways, TV has become a necessary evil. People love to watch it, although they know that there is something inherently wrong with it. Parents, over the years of raising kids, learn that the TV helps keep children pacified while they, the adults, take care of family responsibilities. However, as time passes, they discover that the innocuous digital box, that was effectively keeping their children out of trouble while they washed dishes or put away the clothes, has turned into an addiction. In case you feel TV has got the better of your children, it's time you stepped in, took control of the situation. Below are a few suggestions for watching TV:

- Limit your children's viewing time to no more than two hours per day.
- Identify a list of channels and shows that are acceptable to both, you and your children.

- Ensure your kids do not do homework in front of the TV.
- Do not permit eating while watching TV.
- Set rules for who gets to watch which TV show on a particular day, if you have two or more children with conflicting preferences.
- Make time for viewing TV together with your kids to discuss what they watch.
- Clearly spell out consequences if TV rules are breached and enforce them.

Pocket money: to give or not to give

Pocket money is often a source of confusion for parents—should it be given or not? My belief is that once children are old enough to handle money (around 6–7 years), you should provide them with a regular allowance. Keep the amount moderate, but make sure it is consistent. Providing children with an allowance enables them to learn a number of skills, such as how to save money and how to budget. Further, it prevents children from continuously pestering their parents to buy toys and frivolous things whenever their material desires flare up.

Whenever your kids express their desire to get a new doll or the latest video game, you can suggest they pay for it out of their own funds. When you do so, the tables suddenly turn, forcing them to consider whether they can afford what they want or not. If they can't, you can encourage them to save up for it. Then, when they are able to pay for it, they will feel a greater satisfaction as well as a degree of achievement. Try out these tips regarding pocket money:

- There is no correct amount to be given. The key is to use your discretion, and ensure it is not too much—which would tempt them to be irresponsible with it.

- Give notes of smaller value rather than large ones. This way, your kids will be encouraged to take only the amount they need rather than take the larger denomination notes and wind up spending them.
- Give children actual cash rather than holding the money for them and telling them to ask you for it whenever they need it. It is a practical way for them to manage their money, and to physically watch it come and go. If they are more than ten years old, you may wish to open a bank account for them to teach them how to save money.
- Expect that your children will make some poor decisions in spending their money (e.g., buying a toy that they will become bored of quickly). It is better to let them make some small mistakes with their money now, rather than big ones later.
- Ensure you are not giving kids pocket money in order to compensate for not being able to spend quality time with them.
- Encourage your kids to use 10 percent of their pocket money for helping others or for a charitable purpose.

Case study

A father from Bangalore wrote me an email expressing concern about his six year old son, Sarthak. Every time he took his son out, the boy would demand a new toy, a gadget, a candy, a soft drink or some food item from the shops or malls. Since the father was so busy and rarely got to spend time with his son, he started giving in to his child's whims. However, he got disturbed when he noticed that almost immediately after getting whatever he asked for, his son lost interest in it. He would take two sips of the cola or a few bites of the chocolate bar and then throw away the rest. He would play with the toys once, then get bored with them and never play with them again. It was as if he just wanted to get these things for the sake of getting them.

I explained to the man that his son was bitten by the 'materialism bug'—a form of greed that probably developed from seeing so many commercials on TV. The solution I proposed was that the father give his son a regular allowance—and to let him buy these non-essential things with his own money. I told him that he should be extremely strict about the arrangement, and that if his son ran out of money, he should not become soft and give in to his demands to buy something new. Rather, he should remind his son that perhaps he could save up for it or get it the next time from his pocket money. When I spoke to the father some time later, he described how effectively this strategy worked. While his son initially opposed the new sanctions with bouts of crying and hostile behaviour, he eventually learnt not only to handle his money more wisely, but also how to prioritize his spending.

Having an allowance provides kids with an excellent opportunity to learn fiscal responsibility. You can have them keep regular accounts of how much money they have, as well as how they have spent their money. Then, on a weekly or monthly basis, go over their expenditures with them. This is an excellent way to spend quality time with your kids as well as to teach them extremely important life skills related to mathematics and money management.

How do I get my child to follow the rules?

While your rules may look great on paper, they are of little value unless you implement them effectively. You might be surprised to know that, unlike what most people believe, it is more difficult to teach rules to young children than older children. Read on to find out more.

Age does matter

Adults have very complex brains—filled with all types of knowledge and experiences, and possessing the ability to imagine what the future will be like, and even to re-interpret the past. In fact, as grown ups, we spend so much of our waking hours dwelling in memories or dreaming about the future that we are rarely aware of ourselves in the present moment. However, keep in mind that the part of the brain that helps children manage their behaviour (called the pre-frontal cortex, also known as the 'the executive centre') is the last part of the brain to become developed. While the visual, language, and hearing centres of the brain are all in place within the first few years of your children's lives, the executive centre will not reach full maturity until your kids are in their late teens or even early twenties. So, my first bit of advice to you is that teaching your kids to follow various rules, and to demonstrate good behaviour is going to take a lot of time and patience!

Very young kids

Very young children, i.e., who those are in their infancy and toddler years (0–2.5 years) live in an entirely different world: they have a limited ability to understand complex ideas, their memories are not very distinct, and they are largely incapable of projecting into the future. As such, they spend the majority of their time living in the present moment.

Because their perception is so temporal, it is very difficult to teach them rules. Therefore, your best strategy is to provide verbal and bodily signals that indicate when they are going in the right or wrong direction. When you find them becoming restless, angry, or hard to control, it is best to distract them and draw their attention to something else that can cool them down rather than to resort to physical punishment.

Pre-primary

Once children reach three to four years of age, their mental processes become more sophisticated. While their ability to project into the future is still limited, they do have a stronger capacity to reflect on the past. They will be better able to respond to simple rules, especially when they are coupled with routines. (E.g., 'It's nap time. Now we have to talk in a whisper voice.')

Because their bank of memories is now filled with numerous experiences, you can get them to follow rules more easily by reminding them of past events:

- Remember the last time you jumped on the chair and you fell down and got hurt?
- Remember yesterday, when you got dressed on time? Then there was extra time for colouring.

Children of this age also possess the ability to learn from others' examples. For instance:

- Do you remember what happened when Arman threw the rock and that boy got hurt?
- Do you remember how nicely Beena shared her things and everyone was so proud of her?

You can also offer your advice or opinion as an expert, especially providing your own experience:

- I suggest you don't do that, as it will break and you'll be unhappy.
- When I was a little girl, I teased a dog and it bit me. It hurt a lot.

However, advice and your own personal experience might not be nearly as effective as your children's direct experience.

Although there might not be an immediate connection, do your best to explain the reasons behind rules. For instance: 'If you play with your food like that, it will fall on the floor and then I will have to clean it. That will be a lot of work for me and it will make me tired and angry.' Your children still might defy the rule, and go ahead and play with the food and drop it (they will surely test things to check for themselves). However, when they see the outcome as you had explained, they will have learned something, and might be less inclined to behave the same way in the future. In that sense, it is extremely important for you to be consistent in making, implementing, and enforcing the rules.

Primary and above

Once children reach the age group of 5–7, they have enough experience to draw on examples of the consequences of people following and breaking rules. Their executive centres are also sufficiently sophisticated to enable them to vividly and accurately project into the future (although they don't always do so at the right time to avoid mistakes, accidents, or bad behaviour). For children of this age group and above, you should employ the following techniques:

- Ask them to recall the rules. E.g., 'What are the rules about where to put dirty clothes?'

- Ask them to recall previous experiences where they broke or followed the rules. E.g., 'Remember when you tidied up your room so nicely last week?'
- Ask them to recall previous experiences of other children who broke or followed the rules. E.g., 'What happened the last time you didn't follow your study schedule?'
- Ask them to project consequences. E.g., 'What do you think could happen if you keep teasing your sister and you don't let her do her homework?'

Keep in mind that it might be hard for your kids to project too far into the future or to project things in an abstract way. They might only understand more direct associations. For instance, they might not feel much of a connection if you tell them that if they lie, God will punish them in their next birth.

Using rewards to implement rules

On any given day, you have many things you need your children to do. Wake up, brush their teeth, take a bath, get dressed, eat, do their homework, and so on. However, getting children to cooperate can be a trying experience, especially when you are juggling multiple responsibilities, and when there are time constraints. At times, your children will refuse to do what you want, and you have the challenge of figuring out how to get them to oblige. One way is by rewarding them.

However, rewards should be used sparingly and very carefully. You want to ensure the reward is effective—that children learn that their positive behaviour brings positive results. At the same time, you don't want them to become reward addicts so that they only do things when there is a reward attached to it, especially for routine activities such as brushing their teeth or finishing the food on their plate. Parents who frequently use incentives to get their children to do things might be in for a huge shock one day. For anything you might ask your children to do, they may ask, 'If I do it, what will I get?'

Avoid bribing

Be careful not to use rewards as bribes. For instance, 'If you do well on your test, I will give you Rs 100.' This is an out-and-out bribe to do work that they should be doing anyway.

There's a fine line between bribing and rewarding. A bribe is not always a reward, and a reward is not always a bribe. A bribe is an incentive offered before a task to get your children to do something *you* want them to do. A reward is a *privilege* they receive after a task is completed. If your request is something like, 'If you do this for me, I'll do this for you', it is a bribe. If you say something like, 'As soon as you ________, then you will get to ______________', it is a reward.

At the same time, it is important to remember that both you and your children have goals that need to be achieved. You might want your child to put away her clothing. She might want to go outside and play with her friend. However, you should never allow your children to feel that they are doing what you ask of them only to please you. You must make them understand that they are doing those things because it is part of their responsibility—it is something that they have to do for their own betterment.

So, get them to do the things you want them to do first, and get them to delay their own interests until after those tasks are done.

Further, you don't always need to mention anything about a reward ahead of time—you can be spontaneous about it. For instance, if your child receives good marks on her report card, you may decide to take her out for ice cream or to see a film to express how proud you are of her. This celebratory approach implies that when you've done something well, you deserve to feel good about it.

> **Coaching tip:** Your kids will surely try to find ways to get around the tasks that you set out for them. For instance, they may want to play a video game, and you tell them they must first brush, take a bath, get dressed, eat breakfast, and do their homework. They might brush their teeth and then come back to you to see if they can play now. They might do the same thing after they take a bath. However, if you give in, they will learn that they can bend your rules.

Keep in mind that your kids are watching you. They will test you to see how you react to different tactics to avoid fulfilling your demands. You must be serious and consistent. Only then will they understand that they have to finish your tasks before they can do what they want. Ultimately, this teaches delayed gratification and responsibility—that in life, we have to take care of our responsibilities first before we can enjoy ourselves.

Rewards and punishment

Rewards are effective if the reward is something your kids genuinely want or like. If they really enjoy Bally Sagoo, and you take them to one of his concerts to celebrate their success in their exams, they will surely feel it is a celebration worthy of their achievement. On the other hand, taking them to a classical dance show, however fascinating it might be for you, just might not elicit the same response if it is something that doesn't really interest them. It might actually seem a bit of a let-down.

It is also a good idea to link the reward with the activity that they are being rewarded for. For instance, if your daughter has finished reading her first book, you could reward her with another book. However, it should definitely be a book on a topic that she finds interesting, otherwise the gift might seem like a punishment!

When it comes to punishing your child, tread very carefully. The most important part of punishment is getting to the root of the problem, finding out why it occurred, and correcting that problem. Far too often, whenever children misbehave, parents instantly strike back with a punishment. The parents spend little or no time to understand the reason behind why their child cheated on an exam, bunked a class, lied about where they went with their friends, and so on. In the process, a communication gap grows between the parent and child; it becomes harder and harder to discuss problems when they arise, and children will be inclined to lie to avoid further confrontations.

Here are a few guidelines to dole out punishments:

- Ensure that punishments are clearly pre-decided. Avoid assigning punishments according to your whims.
- Make sure the punishment reflects the degree of the mistake. If a child forgets to do a homework assignment, it would be unfair to stop him from watching TV for a month.
- Make sure that punishments are enforceable. Don't threaten your kids with things that you can't follow through with, e.g., saying you'll move out of the house if they continue to fight.
- Be consistent with punishments. If you don't enforce the rules strictly, your children will treat your words as empty threats and will be likely to ignore them.
- When your kids break a rule, get them to admit their fault and accept responsibility for their action in a rational, non-dramatic manner.

- Focus on restitution, i.e., making the wrong right. E.g., Apologizing, paying for things they have broken (in part or full), helping in cleaning up messes they have made, etc.
- You may decide for a loss of a privilege, e.g., the loss of all or part of allowance for a period of time. When restitution is done, you can then restore that privilege.

Should you raise your hand on your child?

It happens. Children misbehave again and again despite their parents' best attempts to get them to behave correctly. But, when the adults run out of patience and don't know what to do, they resort to one of the easiest and (seemingly) effective solutions: a slap, a spank on the bottom, or any other similar type of physical response.

While physical punishment may have an immediate effect in curbing negative behaviour, it does far more damage than good in the long run. Firstly, it teaches that violence is an acceptable way to express feelings of anger. In time, your children will learn that when they are angry, they also have the right to hit others. Secondly, it does not really solve the problem. A child's bad behaviour may be due to many reasons, which, if you do not uncover, will resurface again and again. Thirdly, children may forget about the behaviour that brought about the beating, and instead, focus on demonizing you. In the process, they will justify their actions, then think of how to avoid getting caught the next time rather than correcting that behaviour. Here are five things to think about before you hit your child:

1. Always remember that you are the parent, the idol that the child seeks to emulate.

2. When your children misbehave, try to identify the root cause of the misbehaviour and find ways to rectify that problem.
3. Ensure that your children get enough attention from you and other family members. Misbehaviour is often a result of not getting enough parental love and attention.
4. Before reacting impulsively, give yourself and your children a chance to settle down. It's often advisable that you leave the room, or have them sit in another room until the heated emotions cool off. Then, discuss the problem rationally and arrive at a solution.
5. Physical abuse puts a check on the bad behaviour temporarily but does not teach your child the correct behaviour. Focus instead on the behaviour you would like to see.

Get them to see the light

The whole point of scolding and punishment is to get children to realize their mistakes. So, choose your response to their misbehaviour carefully and be sure to remain consistent.

Keep in mind that at that moment while you are reprimanding them, you might feel terrible from inside—and your child might express powerful feelings of anger toward you. But don't cave in. The moment will pass, and later, your child will respect you more, love you more, and will be better behaved. It will require every ounce of your patience and strength from inside. But you will surely see the results.

Case study

On a train ride from Amritsar to Delhi, I met a young couple and their five year old son, Veer. They seemed to be having a difficult time controlling him. Whenever they would scold Veer, he would run to the grandfather, and the grandfather would take the grandson's side. As a result, the child rarely heeded the parents' wishes.

I explained to them that all children look for an escape route to get out of doing what they don't want to do—and, as parents, they needed to plug those holes. The only solution here was that the father must talk seriously with the grandfather, and get him to support his and his wife's disciplinary decisions. Though the grandfather believes he is just being loving, he is directly undermining the parent's authority. Over time, the child will lose respect for his parents and refuse to listen to them.

Coaching tip: Often parents are angry about something else but take out their frustration by yelling at their children or sometimes even beating them. If you find yourself doing so, afterwards, be humble enough to apologize for your actions and explain why you behaved the way you did.

Rules and beyond

One of the biggest challenges parents face is dealing with their children's fluctuating emotions. When kids are very young, they have almost no emotional coping skills, and are dependent upon their caretakers to create environments that keep them in a good mood. For instance, notice how babies are quick to laugh, and suddenly without notice or apparent reason, start crying and emit shrieks of distress. They oscillate between the two states within seconds, forcing parents to make noises, make faces, or do anything they can think of to pacify their wailing infants.

As children mature, their emotional faculties develop, and they learn how to manage their feelings with a greater degree of personal control. What most parents don't realize, however, is how significant a role they can play in teaching their kids to handle their emotions more effectively. Below are ten things you can do to help increase your kids' emotional skills.:

1. Talk frequently about feelings. Help them build up their 'feelings' vocabulary and language.
2. Identify triggers—things that make them angry. Get them to recognize these triggers, and avoid them before they take hold.
3. Get them to immediately vocalize when they are getting angry and upset.
   E.g., 'I see you look very angry right now. Would you like to tell me how you feel?' The answer might be, 'I feel like I want to break the wall with my hands.'
4. Ask them how else the problem could be solved without hitting or using foul language.
5. Ask them to take a few deep breaths and blow out their anger.
6. Acknowledge their feelings. E.g., 'I understand you are very upset right now. I know how it feels when someone breaks your favourite toy.'
7. Guess what they might be wishing. E.g., 'I bet you wish we didn't have to leave now.'
8. Get them to express their feelings through writing, drawing, painting, poetry, and other forms of art.
9. Let them know that being angry is okay, but expressing anger through violence is not okay.
10. Stay calm. Children's emotions are often dependent on adults' emotions.

Discuss values with your kids

There is a good reason for having rules: to enable people to get along with each other in life. However, children do not or cannot always see the principles or values behind most rules. When you tell them that they should not watch more than two hours of TV per day, the value behind it is that viewing content that promotes materialism is detrimental to their behaviour or spiritual development. Or, when you tell them that they should adhere to their daily schedule, they might fail to infer that following a structured plan is beneficial for their self-discipline and time management. Because the values are not always apparent, it is imperative that you spend time analysing and exploring the various aspects of rules: the rules themselves, the rule-making process, and most importantly, the reasons behind them.

Be a role model

My best bit of advice to parents, when it comes to implementing rules, is to be a role model. Whatever type of behaviour you wish to see, model that. If you expect your children to get up early, then you should be up early. If you expect them to brush their teeth and bathe before eating breakfast, then you should do the same. The brain contains billions of 'mirror cells'—a type of cell that specializes in copying and imitating the actions of others. If you tell children that they cannot eat while watching TV, but you do it yourself, you will have a hard time convincing them to follow your words. They will come to believe that you are being hypocritical and will wind up resenting you for it. Worse, they will probably start following your example.

> **Coaching tip:** Explain to your children that there are often different rules for children and adults, and also give reasons

for it For instance, adults can go out of the house by themselves, while young children can't; adults can stay up later than children, and so on.

Short hand

- Rules enable children to accomplish their goals better.
- There are a variety of areas where rules can be established. Likewise, there are numerous innovative ways to create them. Children of different ages respond differently to rules, based on their mental abilities.
- With regard to rewards and punishments, the best technique is to make punishments fair, consistent and focused on righting the wrong. Never use rewards as bribes.
- Teach children the values behind rules; encourage them to get internally motivated to make the right choices.
- It is important for you to be a role model in both, laying down and following rules.

Law No. 7
Teach your children to practise

In his 2008 best-selling book, *Outliers*, author Malcolm Gladwell discusses what factors lead to someone becoming a success. While most people believe champions are born—that they possess some kind of 'genius genes'—Gladwell offers a different perspective. After researching the lives of dozens of remarkable achievers, he determined that they all had one thing in common—they all accrued 10,000 hours of practice in their respective fields!

Bill Gates and a few of his classmates began their foray into programming when they were hardly thirteen years old. They sought out every possible minute to get on the computer—even sneaking out of their houses in the middle of the night to use the computers at a local college. Consider Sachin Tendulkar, who showed special talent at an early age. While still a pre-teen, he fanned the flame of his skills by waking up daily at 4:00 am to do rigorous physical training, when most of his classmates were fast asleep. Take any personality, such as Hrithik Roshan, Jhumpa Lahiri, MF Hussain, Amitabh Bachchan, or Lata Mangeshkar. Each one of them will acknowledge a natural God given ability for their talent. However, they will also be sure to tell you about the long hours of dedicated work they performed before they achieved a drop of success in their careers. 10,000 hours to be exact.

There are millions of parents in the world who have high aspirations for their kids—they want them to reach the pinnacle of success. But, why is it that not everyone manages to achieve their lofty goals? While some might believe they were not born with the qualities of a champion, the greater likelihood is that they are not practising enough—or not practising the right way.

How to outsmart studies

Your children might spend hours each day hunched over their textbooks, making their best efforts to study their various academic subjects. But be warned: 'studying' does not equal 'learning'. The real question you need to ask is: Are they practising *hard* or are they practising *smart*? Practising hard means that your children spend a lot of time and energy with their books. It probably also means they are using inefficient methods of practice, learning very little in that time period, and forgetting what they have learned very quickly. Practising smart means using efficient methods of studying—studying for shorter amounts of time, using less energy, and remembering more information for a longer period of time. As we go through this chapter, keep in mind our goal: practising smart!

Get your kids into the 'Learning Zone'

To learn effectively, your children need an environment that is conducive to learning. They must also be in the right frame of mind to learn. I call this place 'the Learning Zone'—a physical and mental space where learning can really happen.

Physical Learning Zone

The Physical Learning Zone refers to the physical place or places where your children study. This could be their bedroom, a study room, the living room, the dining room, etc. Here are five tips to create a conducive Physical Learning Zone for your child:

1. The space should be well lit.
2. There should be a flow of fresh air.

3. Make sure it is not too hot or too cold.
4. Provide a bottle of water close at hand.
5. Ensure that there are no distractions (TVs, crying babies, guests, etc.).

It is almost always better if your children can study in a separate room so they can concentrate better. However, if this is not possible and they have to study in common areas, ensure that there is a schedule that is made clear to everyone in the house, and that others will not play TV, make noise, or create distractions during that time.

Mental Learning Zone

The Mental Learning Zone is a state of mind, where your children have the right amount of stress (good stress, that is), and where learning levels are at their highest.

In order to get your children into the Mental Learning Zone, ensure that:

- they are not overstressed
- they are not understressed (i.e., unmotivated or bored)
- if they are overstressed, help them identify the cause and remove it

Instant solutions for overstress

1. Studying for too long	Take a break
2. Lack of oxygen	Drink water, stretch
3. Thirsty	Drink water
4. Hungry	Eat fruit, nuts or natural, energizing snacks
5. Tired eyes	Take a break, wash the eyes, do palming

Other solutions can include:

- playing music
- taking a walk/exercizing

As a parent, help your children to become aware of their own Learning Zones so that they can keep themselves in the most ideal state for learning for as long as they can. Whether it's their physical environment or mental state, they must learn how to remove distractions to maximize the amount of learning that takes place in a study session.

> **Coaching tip:** Make a checklist with your kids and rate the quality of their study space. Have them identify possible shortcomings or distractions they face and make a plan to improve their Learning Zone.

Schedule your study

The 5th Law taught us about the importance of planning—creating plans to help children achieve their goals. Planning is also extremely important when it comes to studies. If your children can learn how to organize their studying time, they will absorb much more information in the same amount of time.

In the same way that your children have made schedules for their daily routines, have them make a separate weekly calendar for their studies. In this, they should include details of which subjects they will cover. Below is a real life example of a study schedule in the daily routine of a student of Class 9:

6:00 am:	Wake up
6:00 am–7:30 am:	Get ready for the school
7:30 am–8:00 am:	Catch school bus and go to school
8:00 am–2:00 pm:	At school
2:00 pm–2:30 pm:	Come home by school bus
2:30 pm–3:00 pm:	Change clothes and have lunch
3:00 pm–3:30 pm:	Watch TV
3:30 pm–5:30 pm:	Do homework

5:30 pm–6:30 pm:	Go to dance class (Monday, Tuesday and Wednesday)/Play cricket/football with friends (Thursday, Friday and Saturday)
6:30 pm–7:30 pm:	Watch TV
7:30 pm– 8:00 pm:	Play/free time
8:00 pm–8:30 pm:	Eat dinner with the family
8:30 pm–9:30 pm:	Finish homework
9:30 pm–10:00 pm:	Read a book
10:00 –	Go to sleep

Make sure your children keep their study schedule in an easy-to-view place such as in their bedroom or along with other timetables near the place that they study.

Study sessions, blocks, and breaks

When it comes to study time, children often sit for long hours with their books open in front of their faces in the belief that they are studying, and with the hope that they will learn a lot while they are in this 'study mode'. However, keep in mind that just because they are in a 'study position' it doesn't mean they are really studying. A child might sit down for a span of two hours, though be attentive for only 20 minutes during that time. That means that more than an hour and a half is being wasted!

Once a student of Class 10 emailed me to ask how many hours she should study per day. I explained that it's not the amount of time you study. It is the amount of time that you can *focus* while studying. If you can stay focused with full concentration for eight hours a day, then, technically, you can study eight hours a day (though I wouldn't advise it!). But, if you can stay focused for only two hours a day, then you should study for only two hours. So how many hours should your children study daily? For however long they can concentrate. And that is a question only *they* can answer.

One way you can help your children be more efficient is by helping them organize their study time in the following manner:

Study Session				
Study Block	Break	Study Block	Break	Study Block
(15 min)	(3–5 min)	(15 min)	(3–5 min)	(15 min)

- Have them create a 'study session'. This would be a lengthy period of time during which the child will study. It could be for one hour or two hours, depending upon the age and ability of the child.
- Within each study session, have your kids create 'study blocks'. These are periods of uninterrupted study time of about 10–20 minutes each.
- Ensure the children take 3–5 minutes' breaks between each study block.
- Let kids take longer breaks between individual study sessions—at least 20–30 minutes.

The 'funda' of breaks

It is important for your kids to take breaks between study blocks and between study sessions. The reason is that it gives the brain not just a chance to rest, but also an opportunity to sort and assimilate newly-learned information. Taking rest is akin to letting food simmer. After you cook something, you turn off the gas and let the food simmer for 5–10 minutes, during which time the spices have a chance to get absorbed into the food. In the same way, taking a break between study blocks lets the information get absorbed into your child's neural networks.

Below are a few tips you can ask your children to adopt to help them increase their concentration:

- Ensure there are no distractions (refer to the Learning Zone concept).
- While in a study block promise yourself that you will keep focused on the lesson, and that you won't think about other things.
- Have a drink of water.
- Change your position so you are more comfortable.
- Stretch in three ways: 1) Put your hands and arms behind your back, 2) Rotate the shoulders, and 3) Rotate the head in circles. Each can be done for 30 seconds.
- Do deep stomach breathing for 30 seconds. Wait 30 seconds more. Then get back to studying. It's best to do deep breathing right after stretching.
- Remind yourself of your goals so that you can motivate yourself to bring your attention back on track.

Case study

A sixteen year old girl, Samiya, once sent me an email explaining that she was unable to study for more than 30 minutes at a time. She needed a break of at least an hour before she could sit down to study again.

I explained to her that everybody was different and had their own levels of stamina, and that there was nothing wrong with her. She just needed to build up her endurance. Her main problem was that she was trying to study for 30 minutes at a single stretch—and that is a long time for most kids to concentrate! So I recommended that she make a 30 minute study session consisting of study blocks that were 7 minutes each, with breaks in between of 3 minutes. I then suggested that she gradually increase the duration of her study block time from 7 minutes to 8 minutes, and so on. I also reminded her to stay well hydrated while studying by drinking plenty of water, and doing deep stomach breathing during her breaks. After following my advice for two weeks, she was easily able to increase her study blocks to one hour, and was able to memorize much better than before.

Clear starts and stops

When your children do their study sessions, be sure they clearly mark the beginning and the end of each study block. They can do so by making a mental note or by speaking a few sentences aloud stating the block has begun and listing the points to be covered in the block, and doing the same when a block is finished. Having clear starts and stops for each study block significantly boosts the memory, as it assists the brain in organizing and storing the new information, and helping to retrieve it during recall.

It's wise to revise

A critical part of the learning process is revision. Revision is to studying what extra coats are to painting. If you are painting a room and you want the paint to be lustrous and to last long, you have to put on many coats of it. In the same way, you need to revise information numerous times in order for that information to become embedded in your mind. Below are some tips about revision that will help your children get all that information to stick!

Get them to repeat, repeat, repeat

When I was young, I used to have a guitar teacher. He would tell me, 'You should not go to the next part of the song until you can play the first part three times in a row without pausing and without making a mistake. If you can do this, you can be more confident that you have mastered that particular part.' Apart from music, I have also learned to apply this principle to learning of all kinds—learning of language, maths, and so on.

While much is said against the 'ratta ratta ratta' method of teaching, there is actually a lot of wisdom behind the use of repetition during practice. Repetition forces you to internalize whatever you are learning. Often, learners go on to the next topic before they've reached some level of mastery over the previous one, and find that when they return to that topic, they have gaps in their memory.

The 24-hour rule

Did you know that people forget 80 percent of what they have learnt within 24 hours? As such, your children should learn to revise freshly-learned material within a day.

Make sure your children keep at least 50 percent of their study time for revising. Most kids spend the majority of their time studying, and leave barely 5–10 percent of their time for revision. Keep in mind that revision is just as important as studying.

> **Coaching tip:** Revising is very much like putting water on newly-laid cement. If you've ever seen people lay a roof with cement, you'll notice that the next day, and for many days after, they take hoses and spray water on it. This makes the cement more dense, and when it dries fully, the cement becomes extremely strong. Revision has the same effect on memory. Keep this analogy in mind, and get your kids to 'water their cement' with early and frequent revision of the topic.

Methods of revision

Here are some tips your kids can use while revising. They will help them learn more information, in less time, and retain it for longer periods of time.

Flash cards will help them revise in a flash

Flash cards are a great way to help kids revise their academic lessons. They can be used for vocabulary, definitions, equations, historical facts, and for just about any and every subject. You can buy index cards from a stationery shop, or your children can create them by cutting up chart paper. If your kids are using them to learn new vocabulary, they can write the word on one side of the card and the definition on the other side. Here are a few ways to use flash cards effectively:

- Tell your kids to start with a manageable number of cards (e.g., 10–15).
- Have them flip through the cards to test themselves and to be quizzed by others.
- Once they feel they have mastered certain cards, they can keep those cards in one pile. They can keep a separate pile for cards they are having trouble with and move these cards to the mastered pile once they are confident.
- Let them come up with their own ideas and games of how they can learn with the flash cards.

Let me share one flash card learning method I love to use: Start with three flash cards—let's say, each of which contains a word and its definition. Lay them out in front of you. Point to the first one, say the word and its definition. Then point to the second one, and do the same, followed by the third card. Now, mix them up, add one new card, and repeat saying the term and definitions for each card, including the new one. Add another card to the pile and repeat the process. Continue till you reach about fifteen cards.

Flash cards are handy because your kids can take and use them anywhere: on their way to and from school, in between class periods, or when they go to a relative's home for a visit. Whenever they have a few free minutes, they can just pull them out and revise.

It makes sense to use all senses

When it comes to learning, especially academic content, students usually do so by reading their textbooks and class notes silently to themselves. However, neuroscience shows us that the more intense a learning experience is—which makes use of all senses—the greater the chances of remembering it. Make your children try out these three tips on how to use their senses while learning:

1. Saying content out loud while reading. Be sure to vary the volume (loud, medium, soft, whisper).
2. Using bodily movement, such as hand gestures.
3. Singing or dancing. (It might sound silly, but watch what happens when your children choreograph their own dance that represents the process of photosynthesis.)

Many students ask me about how to prepare for exams. One frequent problem concerns last minute preparation, or rather, cramming.

Believe it or not, the brain likes a little bit of stress, that is, just enough to make the task at hand a good challenge. So, when children hear there's going to be a test, the small amount of stress gets them motivated to study. However, when kids wait until the last moment to prepare, their stress levels skyrocket—and the brain does *not* like that. In fact, excessive stress makes the brain less capable of learning and memorizing new things. Therefore, ensure your kids start studying as soon as possible for exams so they can avoid cramming. On the evening before the exam, ensure they go to bed early so they are well rested—discourage them from staying up late, or waking up early to continue studying or revising. There is little they will be able to learn at that point. They are infinitely better off getting the extra rest rather than stressing themselves out, and spoiling their performance in the exam because their mind is worn out.

Getting involved—the coach makes all the difference!

When I was in school, I played on the football team for a few years. Unfortunately, our team had a terrible record—for ten years, we constantly finished at the bottom of our division—never making it to the finals a single time. Each year, we worked hard and maintained positive attitudes, yet, despite our best efforts, we were never able to come out of our decade-long losing streak.

Then one year, we got a new coach—and everything changed. During pre-season preparations, he worked extremely hard with us, teaching us entirely novel ways to practise. He introduced all types of new techniques and ensured we utilized every minute of our practice time effectively. It was no surprise that in his first year as our new leader, our team won every game of the season—an undefeated record of 9–0. At the end of the season, we made it to the finals, and though we lost there by a narrow margin, everyone on our team felt like champions—the entire year's experience was a miraculous transformation for all of us.

What I learned in that year is something that applies to every coach and every parent. It is not enough to have capable, motivated players on your team. And it is not enough for the coach to show interest at only the beginning and end of the season. As the life coach of your kids, you need to assist them in their practice throughout the year, regularly checking on them and pushing them to achieve their potential. Research shows that your active interest in your children's studies has a *direct and significant* impact on how well they will perform. You cannot just leave the responsibilities to their schoolteachers or tuition teachers.

Just three more

One of the responsibilities of coaches is to know how hard to push their players to help them reach their potential. If you don't push your kids hard enough, they are likely to underachieve. And if you push them too hard, they can become extremely stressed out, and suffer from physical and emotional problems. Here is a simple technique you can use to increase their endurance, i.e., to increase the amount of time they can concentrate, and their ability to work by themselves. It's called the 'Just Three More' technique.

Whenever your children are studying, and they express to you that they want to stop studying because they are tired, tell them to do 'just three more', e.g., read just three more pages, answer just three more questions, solve just three more equations, and so on. By pushing them a little further, you enable your kids to increase their study stamina. If you push them to study for another 30 minutes or to answer ten more questions, there are strong chances they will not have enough will-power to do so, and they will give up quickly. Once they complete those three and they come back to you, you can try to convince them to do 'just three more' again. You can also adapt the 'just three more' technique based on the circumstance and your child's age and abilities, making it 'just one more', 'just five more', and so on.

Many parents complain that they do not have sufficient time to help their children with their studies. Even if you don't have much time, try to spend small but consistent amounts of time with them. For instance, set aside a fixed amount of time each day that you will dedicate to your child's studies and personal development. Just 10 or 15 minutes per day of your *active* interest in their lives can have a powerful impact on helping them reach their potential. Be sure to check their daily diaries to see which homework assignments have been given, and that they are completing them. It's not necessary you understand the subject matter, but it is important that you see they are keeping up with their schoolwork.

Teach them to get feedback fast!

Whenever we set out to achieve something, we use feedback to help us know if we're on track. Sometimes it comes from others, e.g., a teacher, a parent, or a friend; other times, it comes from within—we are confident about what we've done, and it just 'feels right'. Whether other-directed or self-directed, feedback is critical to the learning process.

As a parent, you need to teach your children the importance of getting feedback in whatever they are learning—and to *get it fast*. The reason is that if you make a mistake and keep going, the brain's neurons register that knowledge or action as correct until further notice. The longer your children believe that thing to be correct, and the more they go on doing or thinking about it in the wrong way, the harder it becomes to correct it.

You might have experienced this yourself. You get someone's name wrong from the start. Then, even though they tell you their correct name, you accidentally keep calling them the wrong name again and again. The same is true for anything that children learn. So again, the golden rule is 'get feedback fast'.

When giving feedback to your kids, it's important to remember that it comes in different flavours. Most parents are concerned with negative feedback, that is, letting kids know when they have made mistakes or have not done something up to the mark. However, there is also positive feedback—informing your kids when they do something right. Both types of feedback are important, although most parents tend to become obsessed with the mistakes their kids make.

While giving negative feedback, try not to get angry or emotional. Avoid making comments that are demeaning such as, 'Why can't you get it?' or 'I've explained this ten times already!' or 'Why are you so dumb?' Speaking in such a manner causes children to get defensive, angry, or frustrated. This increases stress, crushes their self-esteem, and prevents them from being able to accept your feedback to make the necessary improvements. Therefore, when negative feedback is unavoidable, I strongly suggest you provide some positive reinforcements first to keep your children in a more emotionally accepting state of mind. Then give them the corrective response in a focused and casual manner. For example:

- 'You seem to understand decimals really well. Nice going. However, you need to re-check the answers of your fraction problems.'

When you do give negative feedback, avoid telling them the correct answer straight away. Rather, give them a hint, and provide them with the opportunity to spot the mistake and correct it themselves. For example:

- 'Are you sure everything is correct there?'
- 'I see you were able to conjugate the regular verbs properly. It looks as though you've really got that. However, I see some errors with the irregular verbs.'

If they continue to struggle, try offering additional hints as far as possible rather than giving the answer away:

- 'What do you think is wrong with the word 'teached'?'

There are many children who are not bothered with corrections that their teachers make. They simply view all their mistakes as one big mistake, and move on. Help your children realize that mistakes are an opportunity for them to learn something. When they get back an exam paper, spend time to look at their mistakes, and discuss the same with them. You can help them clear confusions and misconceptions they still might have. If you don't, it is likely that those same confusions and misconceptions will resurface again and again.

Identifying the kind of mistake also helps to identify and solve the problem.

Possible scenarios:

- Your child did not know or understand the concept.
- Your child understood the concept incorrectly.
- Your child understands the concept, but accidentally made a mistake due to distraction, lack of concentration, carelessness, or lack of practice.

As a parent, you need to treat each case differently. If your child did not know or understand the concept at all, you need to start right at the beginning and explain it. If he understood the concept incorrectly, you should ask him to explain what he has understood. Don't just lecture him about the right way. Only when you understand his misconception, you can better help him clear it. With regard to accidental mistakes, spend less time talking about the topic, and more time on encouraging your child to concentrate or practise.

While it is important to ensure your children get feedback as quickly as possible, you also want to ensure they are not just being lazy. Ensure your children do not overdo the urge to get feedback *too* frequently. While very young children might want your inputs after each problem, try to encourage them to do 2–3 problems before seeking help; then slowly increase the number. You can also teach them to build their endurance by having them put a question mark next to the problem they are facing; then after a period of time, they can come to you and clear their doubts in one go.

> **Coaching tip:** If your kids ask too many questions, try giving them a question limit. Provide them with chits of paper and explain that for each question they ask, they have to give you one chit, and that when the chits are finished, they can't ask any more questions. This will get them to be more judicious about the questions they ask. Start by giving them more chits. Slowly reduce the number so that your children learn to become more specific when asking for help.

How to perfect the art of practice

One last point I would like to mention is the importance of attitude during practice. It's not enough that your children practise half-heartedly, just for the sake of practising. Their whole being must be engaged in learning. In Vedic terms, such practice is called sadhna, which indicates not a mere mechanical repetition of actions, but rather, a profound development of the individual through committed effort. Those who achieve great things in their lives are not the ones who just 'go through the motions' with their hearts and minds elsewhere, but rather, the ones who give it their all.

Short hand

- Create the right atmosphere by making Physical and Mental Learning Zones.
- Make a study plan that enables your kids to stay on top of their work. This is important to avoid the stress of last minute studying.
- Help your children in organizing their study time, which needs to be broken into sessions and blocks, with the right amount of rest in between.
- Teach your children methods to revise in order to solidify what they learn. Play a valuable role as a parent and coach.
- Encourage them to practise with a positive attitude and with complete commitment.

Law No. 8
Teach your children to play

As I sit down to write this chapter, I am gazing out of my office window that overlooks the playground at the Jiva Public School in Faridabad. It is recess time, and hundreds of children zoom about in every direction, like over-stimulated electrons in some volatile molecular experiment. Five boys are aggressively fighting to get possession of a basketball; three girls are skipping rope in perfect synchronization; one boy is chasing another at full speed and they are both screaming and laughing wildly; two teams of girls are playing kho kho; a boy who has fallen is crying and a friend is consoling him and escorting him off the field.

Despite the somewhat random appearance of their movements, and the cacophony generated by their romping about, there is a tremendous amount of learning taking place in this symphony of play. At closer inspection, this recess period is a complete lesson in competition, team spirit, cooperation, physical coordination, timing, strategy, action and consequences, compassion, risk-taking, friendship, and more. In fact, the lessons being learnt in this 30 minute session might have more impact than the civics or geometry lesson they might just have attended.

According to research done by psychiatrist Dr Stuart Brown, the desire to play is a fundamental drive in all intelligent beings—humans, dogs, cats, monkeys, bears—and even ants. Brown explains that play is not gratuitous behaviour meant just for killing time. Rather, it is an activity critical to life that enables individuals to grow and to develop—to learn about their abilities, the physical rules of our world, and the dynamics of social interaction. On top of this, it also improves physical and mental health, significantly reducing stress. In short, play enables humans to learn, adapt and evolve.

Unfortunately, parents' obsession with academic achievement has clouded their perspective on play. When children want to spend time outside, engage in a video game, dance, or paint a picture, parents usually see such activities as useless distractions to their studies. In this chapter, my aim is to get you to think differently about play, so that you see it as a necessity for your children—no different than eating, sleeping or studying. It is my hope that you will soon see to it that they receive a healthy dose of play in their daily schedules so that they can maximize their potential and unleash the inner champion.

What is play?

Play typically refers to activities where the participants take part voluntarily for the sake of amusement and enjoyment. These activities may be done individually or with others, by young and old alike, and may make use of various props or toys. Play may be structured, containing specific goals and rules, sometimes becoming a game, or may be more unstructured and open-ended. These activities may include:

- **Large motor play:** including all types of body movements as in running, jumping, climbing, swinging, and sliding.
- **Small motor play:** playing with small objects and engaging in activities that require physical and mental dexterity such as solving puzzles, sorting objects, stinging beads.
- **Construction play:** a type of play that requires skill and imagination for building structures such as houses, forts, ships, and so on.

- **Role play:** this type of play usually begins with 'Let's pretend...', and evolves into different situations that children have experienced or imagined.
- **Language play:** this is when children make up or change words, rhymes, verses, stories and songs.
- **Arts play:** children integrate all forms of art into their play, using whatever materials are at hand to draw, model, create music, perform puppet shows, and so on. They explore the arts and use them to express their feelings and ideas.
- **Rough and tumble play:** these activities involve physical risk-taking as well as rough-housing, where participants demonstrate aggression within limits so that no one actually get hurt.

Why do we play?

We play for a number of reasons. The first is a desire for companionship. In the course of play, we establish feelings of friendship, belonging, community, and trust. Another reason is to know more about ourselves and how the world works. Through play, we discover how our bodies function—how they can be manoeuvred and how we can master a variety of movements—everything from how to walk, to how to climb a tree. In the process, we also use play to learn how to deal with various objects from rocks to balls to water; through playful experimentation, we learn how to control and manipulate them. We also play to enable us to rehearse for roles we need to play. Young children often imitate their parents— pretending to cook, clean, entertain guests, and so on. Play also enables us to act out our fantasies—just for sheer pleasure, entertainment, and exploration of ideas.

Benefits of play

There are numerous benefits that your children will enjoy

when you ensure that they get enough play in their educational diet. Play:

- fosters interpersonal skills
- teaches the values of fairness and sharing
- improves language skills (as children use language in more complex ways than they do with teachers and in rigid classroom settings)
- makes them smarter
- makes them more creative
- improves problem-solving skills

It has even been shown that there is a correlation between play and success. Dr Stuart Brown has shown that Nobel Prize-winning scientists, business icons, and others with achievement records, have engaged in a significant amount of play during their childhood and even adult lives. He has also stated that individuals who fail to play enough in their childhood tend to be less creative, less capable of learning new things and face more problems in the social and emotional domains.

Kids need a whole lot of play

Why are we playing less nowadays? When play is something so instinctive that even animals indulge in it, why do educators need to be telling parents to get their kids to play more? There are a number of reasons.

First, the modern education system was designed to behave like a factory that would pump kids full of information and skills, which, after twenty years or so, would produce intelligent, capable human beings who would contribute to the Industrial Revolution. Numerous things were eliminated from children's lives, including their exposure to the Arts and play. Instead, education kept weighing down children's already loaded plates each year, and even added a further burden of examinations. Second, in countries such as India, and particularly in urban India, children have become restricted to their homes. Children living in towns and cities hardly get a chance to play outside because there are frequently no sidewalks or parks and roads are dangerous. Third, joint families are on the decline, and as such, there are often fewer people available for kids to play with. Last, TV has largely replaced much of the time that children used to utilize for play.

Unfortunately, we are putting more and more stress on children by increasing the burden of their syllabus, and at the same time, we are denying them the very thing they need to bust that stress: play.

How to make your children's lives more playful

So, what is it that you can do to increase the playful element in your kids' lives? Here are a number of tips you can use:

- Be sure to set aside ample time in your kids' daily schedule for play.
- Ensure they engage in different types of play (individual, interpersonal, role-play, large motor, small motor, etc.).
- Create an environment at home that is conducive to play. Stock up on all sorts of stuff, such as books, toys, board games, puzzles, papers, scissors, crayons, etc.
- Don't be overprotective and try to make their environment devoid of anything dangerous. Keep things balanced.
- Engage your kids in real work from time to time so they get a feeling for responsibility. This will enrich their play time with new ideas and roles to enact.

When I tell parents to engage their children in different types of play, they sometimes complain that their children show no interest in anything other than TV.

One reason for this is that the children might not have been exposed to a variety of play types from a young age and, therefore, have no taste for it. So, my suggestion is to impose a limit on the amount of time children are allowed to watch TV (e.g., 1–2 hours per day) and to schedule specific times for play. Then, offer the children options of which types of play they would like to engage in. In time, their appetite for play will surely increase.

Coaching tip: Help your children identify the activities that best suit their natures, as they will find more success and satisfaction in it.

List of play activities and hobbies

Science

Astronomy
Electronic kits
Radio-controlled vehicles
Rock-collecting
Robotics

Making things

Making musical instruments
Pottery
Sculpture
Film-making
Doll-making
Restoring antiques
Pottery
Painting and drawing
Bracelets
Soap-making
Paper-making
Beadwork and beading
Gardening
Rock-climbing
Bird-watching
Woodwork/carpentry
Candle-making
Cooking
Jigsaw puzzles
Sewing
Scrap-book making
Candle making
Origami
Jewellery-making
Embroidery
Wood-carving
Sports and outdoors
Hiking
Mountain-climbing
Kite-flying

- Cricket
- Tennis
- Badminton
- Martial arts
- Football
- Table tennis
- Basketball
- Horse-riding

Collecting

- Coins
- CD-ROMs
- Books
- Bottles and cans
- Comic books
- Currency
- Toys
- Guitar
- Keyboards
- Sitar
- Collect music like CDs or albums
- Composing music
- Stamps
- Posters
- Movies
- Insects
- Crystals, rocks and minerals
- Fountain pens
- Music
- Drums
- Tabla
- Join a rock band
- Karaoke

Performing arts

- Juggling
- Dancing
- Singing
- Poetry reading
- Puppetry
- Magic tricks
- Acting/drama
- Story-telling

Others

- Reading
- Computer programming
- Keeping an aquarium
- Blogging
- Tie and dye
- Baking
- Photography
- Making websites
- Journalism/writing
- Body building
- Mehendi

Hobbies—turning play into passion

When children are exposed to a variety of play experiences, they will inevitably find some that really tickle their fancy. When their spark of interest turns into a flame, that is your clue to encourage them to take their interest to the next level and turn it into a passion. You can do so by helping them find a hobby, an activity on which they can spend extended amounts of time. There are literally thousands of hobbies your kids can choose from, many of which you can see on the previous page. Here are ten reasons why your children should have a hobby. A hobby:

1. **Increases motivation:** When an interest grows into a passion, children discover a new sense of purpose in life.
2. **Enhances skills:** Children can build a wide range of skills from their hobby—motor skills, language skills, and others related to their Multiple Intelligences.
3. **Boosts confidence:** When children spend time in their hobby and become 'good at it', their self-esteem automatically increases.
4. **Encourages reading:** While learning about their hobby, kids will be much more inclined to take their own initiative to read up on it—things like instructions, the history of that activity, or biographies of people from that field.
5. **Expands their knowledge and interest in studies:** When children begin to see connections between their hobby and their academic subjects, their interest level in their studies rises.
6. **Increases creativity:** Hobbies cultivate the creative spark and promote new ways of thinking.
7. **Increases concentration and attention:** When children are driven to learn because of their passion, they will spend longer amounts of time concentrating on their hobby, which enhances their overall ability to concentrate.
8. **Reduces the amount of time they watch TV:** Kids will gladly sacrifice TV time to work on a hobby-related activity.

9. **Reduces stress:** Hobbies enable children to forget about their daily tensions, and give their mind a much-needed refreshing break.
10. **Can lead to a career:** Many people's obsession with a hobby ultimately leads them into a profession that builds on that interest.

Coaching tip: Be prepared to make some space for your child's hobby. Certain hobbies require children to build, use glue, paint, cut, and generally create disorder. Designate a specific area where your children can engage in their hobby without excessive fear that they are going to break, damage, or spoil something that will make you angry. After all, experimentation and making a mess are a necessary part of the creative process!

Let's play on!

You need to teach your child how to play so that he can make the most of it.

A playful attitude

No matter what type of play your kids get involved in, make sure they realize that the most important thing is that they maintain the spirit of play. If they become too obsessed about winning, by what others think, or about someone else's ability to do something better than them, they will find it difficult to become immersed in play and to derive the benefits that it has to offer them. In such cases, take some time out to help them realize that their goal is to improve and enjoy themselves. It is here that you have to remind them of the well-known proverb: 'It isn't whether you win or lose, but how you play the game'.

Team spirit

When your children play with others, they get an excellent opportunity to learn valuable social skills. This is especially true when it comes to team play. Help them recognize the unique qualities each player brings to the team, and find ways to engage everyone's talents in the best way possible. Such skills become a huge asset later on in their professional lives—as managers, administrators, owners of companies, etc. Further, it teaches them the critical lesson that no matter which situation they might find themselves in, they should find their niche.

Here are ten important lessons related to being a team player that you can share with your children:

1. **Play by the rules:** Rules are there for a purpose—to enable everyone to enjoy playing.
2. **Give everyone a chance to play:** It is no fun if only a few people dominate the game and others don't get an opportunity. Remember the film 'Chak De India' and 'pass the ball'.
3. **If you take something out, put it back:** Teach your kids to be responsible for keeping and storing any game or play paraphernalia. Don't let them leave their play things around for you to put away.
4. **Pull your own weight:** Don't let others do all the work while you enjoy yourself at the cost of their efforts.
5. **If you made a mess, clean it up:** If you spilled something, broke something or made the place untidy while you were playing, clean it up yourself. Don't wait for someone else to do it.
6. **Respect others' time:** Group efforts require planning and coordination. Be punctual and show up when you are supposed to.
7. **Appreciate others:** Praise others for their contributions and unique qualities that they bring to the activity.
8. **Win with grace:** Give credit to everyone who

contributed to your success and don't taunt opposing players.

9. **Lose with grace:** No one likes a sore loser. Accept defeat with humility and aim to improve the next time around.
10. **Have fun:** Don't ever forget that the most important part of play is to enjoy yourself!

Coaching tip: Teach your children that when people are behaving in an unfair or improper manner while playing, they have the right not to participate; if they feel something is wrong or unjustified, they should stand up for themselves and refuse to take part in it.

Case study

A young mother contacted me about her four year old son who often played very aggressively, and she was worried about how to handle it. I advised her that play-fighting is a natural behaviour among children, and researchers believe it actually plays a vital role in their social and emotional development. At the same time, kids respond differently to certain types of rough-and-tumble play. After some discussion, she agreed to set special times for play-fighting and established clear rules for the activity (e.g., no hurting, no hitting in sensitive places, stopping when the other child says he has had enough, etc.). She supervised the bouts, ensuring that the children present wanted to be involved in that type of play, and that the play-fighting didn't turn into real fighting. As a result, she found that her son was better able to focus his aggressive energy, and was less likely to become aggressive outside the structured rough-and-tumble sessions.

Your turn to play

It's not enough to merely get your kids to play more. You should also set a good 'play example' by regularly playing with them yourself. You can do so by participating with them in games or sports, or even jointly getting involved in a hobby with them. Whatever you decide to do, remember that time spent together in play creates an incredible opportunity for bonding. It will help establish powerful emotional ties with your children that will enable you to remain close to them throughout your lives.

Many parents complain that they are unable to connect with their children—that they have nothing in common with them and that they seem to live in separate worlds. It can be frustrating when you feel you cannot keep up with them—the technologies they use, the jargon they speak, the music they listen to, and the clothes they wear. Unfortunately, if the spaces between you and your kids grow too far apart, it becomes hard to communicate, and at times of crisis, it is impossible to bridge those gaps. Remember that bonds need to be built over time, and playing together regularly is one way to keep those ties alive and strong.

Finally, by involving yourself in playful activity, you keep your own brain active. Research shows that adults who remain playful and who keep their minds engaged in novel activities tend to retain their memory better as they age. A regular dosage of daily play will keep your grey matter fit well into your old age.

Case study

A woman from Mumbai contacted me because her daughter Sakshi, who had recently become a teen, was not communicating with her. Whenever she came home from school, the girl would immediately go to her room and lock her door, emerging for meals and little more. The mother was worried because her daughter was spending too much time on the phone, text messaging, using

Facebook, and watching TV. And she had started wearing clothes that she, the mother, did not find appropriate.

I suggested that instead of confronting her daughter directly (which would likely have adverse effects), she should try finding some common activity that they could do together. The woman used to be a jewellery designer, though after marriage she had given it up. Now, she decided to revive her hobby, and invited her daughter to join her. The girl was delighted by the prospect of being able to increase her collection of fashion accessories. She quickly became fascinated as she worked with the array of beads, glass, and wire, and subsequently, developed a new-found appreciation for her mother's creative talent. In time, mother and daughter established a much better bond that opened the doorway for them to communicate and share their feelings openly with each other.

Short hand:

- Children must have a substantial amount of their day set aside for engaging in activities that let them move their bodies, manipulate objects, role-play and use their imagination.
- You are unknowingly working against your children's future success if you have been pushing them harder and harder to concentrate on their studies and denying them opportunities to play.
- Get your kids to incorporate more playful experiences in their daily schedules as this will do wonders for their social skills, creativity, and sense of confidence.
- Because play so often involves others, it is an excellent opportunity for children to learn how to play fairly and be a team player. Such skills will enable them to

rise to great heights in their lives—both, personally and professionally.

- Kids need to realize the power of attitude in everything they do. By maintaining a playful attitude, they will be able to find enjoyment in just about any activity they engage in.

Law No. 9
Teach your children the tricks of the trade

I'll never forget the first time I tried to make a chapatti. Like most beginners who attempt to take the small lump of dough and roll it into a perfect circle, I struggled and strained and wound up with something that looked more like the map of India. I tried again and again, but to no avail. I was simply unable to attain the roundness that seemed to come so effortlessly to my friend's wife.

'The trick,' she told me, 'is to roll your wrists gently in circles and to make the chapatti also follow the same circular movements on the rolling board.'

After she revealed the secret behind the technique, I watched her again carefully. This time I could see how the circular motions rolled out the dough into perfect disc shapes. My next few shots at it were still far from perfect, but after my 8th or 9th attempt, things took a turn for the better. I was no longer trying to force out a round chapatti; the dough was effortlessly moving on its own and gently taking on a circular shape. That's all it took—just one bit of advice, one small trick—and the door to making a chapatti was unlocked for me.

A trick is a difficult manoeuvre which seems amazing, magical, and impressive to onlookers. We find similar 'tricks' in many areas of life, including sports, maths, music, gardening, sewing, and computer graphic design. Interestingly, there are even tricks to learning—methods of memorization that enable you to quickly learn large amounts of information—and to retain that information for longer periods of time.

There are a number of benefits of learning tricks. They:

- Enable you to improve your performance.
- Help you save time and energy.
- Help you gain an edge when competing against others.
- Are fun.

Because tricks are so integral to gaining mastery in any field, and because these days children are challenged to memorize large volumes of information, I have dedicated one Law of Learning specifically to 'learning tricks'. These are techniques that your children can use for any of their subjects. They may also apply them to other areas of their daily life such as dance, drama, giving speeches, and so on. You'll find that learning these tricks is not that difficult, and can actually generate interest that might have been missing earlier.

Acronyms

One helpful way of remembering information is to use acronyms. Acronyms are words that are created from other words, using the first letter of each word. For instance, you probably recall the acronym you used in school to recall the colours of the rainbow—VIBGYOR, i.e., Violet, Indigo, Blue, Green, Yellow, Orange, and Red, or the order of operations—BODMAS, i.e., Brackets, Orders, Division, Multiplication, Addition, and Subtraction. If your children are having a difficult time remembering lists or groups of terms, suggest they create acronyms out of the lists. Here's one that a student from my school made up to remember the different types of simple machines: LIPSWAX (lever, inclined plane, pulley, screw, wedge, axel and wheel).

They can also make acronymic sentences, i.e., creating a memorable sentence that uses the first letter of each word. For instance, to remember the eight planets, they can easily remember My (Mercury) Very (Venus) Elegant

(Earth) Mother (Mars) Just (Jupiter) Served (Saturn) Us (Uranus) Noodles (Neptune).

Visual associations

Another trick that your kids can use to help them remember things more easily is to use visual associations—making pictures that can be linked to the words or concepts.

The key to making successful associations is that they should be:

- Clear images
- Funny
- Exaggerated. Make things really big, really small, etc.

If you don't make the images clear, funny or exaggerated, you will forget them quickly—they just won't stick.

Coaching tip: If there are many words to be remembered, it is helpful when you turn associations into stories.

Last year, I was working with a group of students who wanted to learn some tricks to help them memorize better. I asked them to bring me a lesson they thought was particularly tough. One student from Class 9 took out his biology textbook and showed me a lesson on kidneys. He then showed me this scary-looking page with extremely detailed diagrams and dozens of labels made up of complicated words—Nephron tubules, Malpighian tubules, renal tubules, collection tubules, Bowman's capsule, glomerulus, Henle's loop, and so on. I looked at the magnitude of it all, took a deep breath, summoned my creativity, and launched into a session of 'association'.

'Okay, Nephron. What does it sound like? How about nephew? So now we have to think that the kidney has a nephew. A pig wearing a mala (flower necklace)–malpighian.'

'What does 'renal' remind you of?' One student said, 'A person named Rena.' 'Okay, so imagine Rena chasing a pig.' By now everyone was cracking up. 'And what is she doing? She's chasing the pig because it's stealing and collecting her test tubes—thousands of them. So what does she do? She calls a man with a bow and arrow to shoot tranquilizer capsules at the pig (Bowman's capsule). He hits the pig and it runs into a fashion show where there are all these glamorous (glomerulus) people and everyone starts screaming. The pig then runs out into an amusement park to meet his accomplice, the hen who is riding a rollercoaster and doing a loop, and laying an egg each time she does one loop (Hen lay loop, i.e., Henle's Loop), and so on.'

At this point, all the children were doubling up with laughter. I asked them how they felt. Tired? No way—they were all energized!

> **Coaching tip:** Make sure your kids understand the content. I know of examples where kids have written the associated words in tests—they are not likely to get any points for writing 'glamorous' instead of 'glomerulus', or writing that the kidney is responsible for helping hens lay eggs!

Spelling tricks

English is a crazy language. Shouldn't 'laugh' be spelt as'laff'? And why is there a 'gh' in 'taught'? Shouldn't it be 'taut'? Kids have a tough time remembering how words are spelt because the English language is a khichadi, made up of many other languages, including Celtic, German, Latin, and French. In order to help your kids remember the correct spellings, here are a number of tricks you can teach them.

Linguistic technique

Here is famous poem that helps remember when to use 'ie' and when to use 'ei':

i before e, except after c
Or,
when sounding like a
As in neighbour and weigh

This poem helps kids remember to drop the 'silent e' when adding 'ing' to a word:

When -ing comes to stay,
little e runs away.

(e.g., 'take' becomes 'taking' and 'make' becomes 'making'.)

Visual technique

Look for small words in larger words.

E.g., The words 'sat' and 'fact' are in 'sat-is-fact-or-y'

Auditory technique

Pronounce words by breaking them into chunks or syllables and exaggerating the different parts.

E.g., Feb - ru - a - ry, Wed - nes - day, in - de - pen - dent

Bodily technique

Use your finger to trace the spelling of words in the air or on the desk.

You can also try writing the word on pieces of paper. Then rearrange the pieces to 'make' the word.

Coaching tip: Remember not to overdo tricks. It is essential that your children master the basics of whatever they are learning. Tricks are valuable as extensions of whatever they are learning.

Memorizing long answers and speeches

Here are some tips you can teach your children that will help them memorize questions that have long answers. The method is also helpful for remembering speeches or lines from a play.

Backward build-up method

- Start by reading the first sentence out loud. (e.g. To be or not to be, that is the question).
- Ensure you get the rhythm of the sentence.
- Say the last word of the sentence (e.g., ...question).
- Say the second last word of the sentence followed by the last word (e.g., ...the question).
- Say the third last word of the sentence, the second last word, and then the last word (e.g., ...is the question).
- Say the fourth last word, then the third last, the second last, and finally, the last word (e.g., ...that is the question).
- Keep doing this until you get the whole sentence.

Word elimination method

- Write the entire sentence (e.g., To be or not to be, that is the question).
- Eliminate one word from the sentence (other than the first). You can do this by drawing over the word with a marker. Then say the sentence, adding in the missing word (e.g., To be or not to be, that is the question).
- Eliminate one more word. Then repeat the sentence, adding the two missing words (e.g., To be or not to be, that is the question).
- Continue the process until all the words are eliminated.

First letter method

- Write the first letter of each word in the sentence (e.g., T b o n t b, t i t q).
- Look at the clue letters, say each word, filling in the missing letters.

- Delete the last letter of the sentence and say the sentence (e.g., T b o n t b, t i t...).
- Then delete the second to last letter, and say the sentence (e.g., T b o n t b, t i...).
- Repeat this until all the letters are deleted.

Mind mapping

An excellent way to help your children remember things more easily is with the help of Mind Maps. Mind Maps are nothing but pictorial representations of information. They are usually centred around a single theme, and may contain words, ideas, and other items that are connected by branches stemming from the key concept. An interesting visual tool, it not only helps children see the relationship between ideas but also enables them to classify information, memorize content, solve problems, brainstorm and take decisions.

Below is an example of a Mind Map related to pollution.

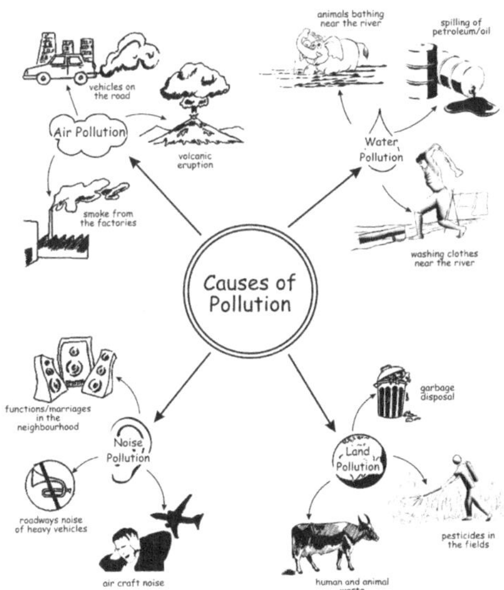

Mind Maps can be made for virtually any subject and topic, including social studies, science, geography, computers, language arts, maths and so on.

To create a Mind Map, have your child take a blank page, and begin by writing the key idea in the centre of the page. He should then identify words or concepts connected to that point, draw branches radiating outward from the centre, and put those related words at the ends of the branches. He can continue the process, creating new branches and ideas from the sub-points. Mind Maps can be used as effective teaching aids as well as revision tools. If your child is having a hard time grasping a concept, try using a Mind Map to explain it more clearly. Or once he's gone through the matter in his textbook, have him create a visual model to demonstrate his genuine comprehension of the ideas and how they fit together.

Encourage your child to have fun with the Mind Mapping process. Let him use coloured sketch pens and create interesting designs that make the ideas and links visually appealing. He can even include images related to the topic. For instance, a Mind Map about different types of transportation could contain pictures of different vehicles connected by lines that look like roads while a Mind Map related to farming and agriculture could have ideas connected by vines or canals, where various sub-points sprout out of the ground or hang off trees inside pieces of fruit.

Encourage them to create their own tricks

Explain to your children that there are tricks for everything in life including cooking, sports, music, skating, and so on. Once your children are comfortable with using various tricks to enhance their learning, they can come up with their own memorization methods. In fact, this is something

I've seen many kids do automatically. However, you first need to model enough techniques and only then encourage them to create their own.

> **Coaching Tip:** To make the code words more memorable, ensure they are funny, exaggerated, and linked somehow to the topic.

Short hand

- There are a number of tricks that your children can use in order to learn things more easily and to remember them for longer periods of time.
- Acronyms help in memorizing lists of words, while associations can be used to remember new words.
- There are numerous techniques, which make use of different kinds of intelligences to help with spelling.
- Multiple Intelligences and Multiple Natures can be dovetailed into whatever your children might be studying—to get their whole beings into the learning process.
- You can explore and discover many more tricks to help your children learn easily. Additionally, encourage your kids to come up with their own unique methods of learning. Once your kids get hooked on to these 'tricks', they are sure to discover a new passion for learning.

Law No. 10
Teach your children to perform like champions

There are many great cricketers in the world, yet among them, Sachin Tendulkar is considered a champion. There are dozens of actors who have achieved tremendous levels of fame, yet Amitabh Bachchan is considered to be in a league of his own. While some would call these illustrious individuals 'winners', actually they are more than winners. They are champions.

Champions are people who are deeply committed to their goals. They do not excel merely for want of fame, or money, or power. They rise to great heights because they focus on giving their best performance each time. If you talk to actors who have worked with Amitabh Bachchan, they will tell you that despite his phenomenal success, he always arrives on time for a film shoot and he always has all of his dialogues memorized. He doesn't behave like a spoilt celebrity, requiring special treatment or care unlike some other actors who throw tantrums when they don't get their particular brand of bottled water. And anyone who has watched Sachin Tendulkar over the years will admit that it is not only his legendary batting skills that make him special, but also his sportsmanship, humility, and generosity.

If your children follow the first nine Laws of this book, they will have made incredible progress in their lives. In this final chapter, we will look at the qualities that distinguish a champion from a winner.

Coaching tip: Be sure to explain to your kids that champions need not only be star athletes or performers. They can also be mothers and fathers who are wholly dedicated to raising their children, teachers who are fully committed to their students' progress, and other such people they encounter in their daily lives who demonstrate devotion to their families, community and professions.

Champions are disciplined

Your children might have short term goals like passing an exam, learning to ride a bicycle, or long term goals like forming a rock band, becoming a top rated chef, running a marathon, developing a cure for cancer, becoming a successful entrepreneur, and so on. They might pursue those goals partly for self-satisfaction, the approval of others, or the sheer enjoyment of the challenge. But, they also most likely pursue them for the special privileges that are associated with them—the fame factor, becoming healthier and more attractive, the pleasure of helping others, the chance to associate with accomplished people, and, last but not the least, acquiring financial resources that will enable them to enjoy material benefits.

Most children look at successful people and want to be like them without knowing what is necessary to achieve it. They are not prepared to put in the extra hours of practice required to master the basic skills, let alone the advanced ones. While they may occasionally dream of bathing in the spoils of success, they are not ready to sacrifice watching TV, hanging out with friends, sleeping late on the weekends, or eating fast food everyday. In short, they are not ready to discipline themselves.

While many of the things that can help one achieve success are not in your children's control (e.g., their genetic abilities or the availability of a superior coach in their school), one thing certainly is: their ability to regulate their time, schedules, and behaviour. When you interact with your kids to discuss their academic or life activities, ensure that their goals are clear, that they have effective plans, and that they create an environment that enables them to concentrate. But most importantly, make sure that the goals have been chosen for the right reasons and not just for the rewards that accompany them.

Once you see that your kids' interests, abilities, and goals are in tandem, stand behind them and root them on. Be a coach and a fan, and provide them with love, support, guidance, and encouragement while they practise. When you see them losing steam, be there to cheer them on and remind them of their goals. (And don't forget to explain Malcolm Gladwell's 10,000 hour principle to them—that people who achieve mastery in their field do so only after spending 10,000 hours working at their craft!)

Champions are passionate

If your son loves cricket, you don't have to chase him to read the latest cricket news, watch the World Cup finals, or meet up with his friends in the afternoon to play a bunch of overs. In fact, the opposite is likely to be true—you'll probably be after him to put down the remote or his bat and get back to his schoolwork and other responsibilities. As we saw in Chapter 3, all human beings have a desire to know and to explore their world. And when they stumble upon something that matches with their interest and nature, the sparks begin to fly.

Keep your eyes open to the things that catch your child's interests, and teach them to nurture that passionate energy that wells up from within. When they become conditioned or used to having something to be passionate about, they will turn that fountain of emotions into something else. You cannot always be certain about what your kids will get hooked onto, but to a large extent, you *can* control the options to increase the chances that whatever they latch onto is valuable, constructive, and conducive to their positive development.

Champions have integrity

Integrity is a quality in people—one that not only implies honesty, but also includes a consistency of values and actions. When people are consistent, they perform reliably, and others come to depend on them—and seek them out. People hire drivers who consistently drive without an accident; hospitals employ surgeons who have the highest degree of success with their procedures; families engage wedding planners who they can count on for ensuring that the most important moment of their children's lives is not botched up because the stage collapsed during the family photo session.

Unfortunately, most parents don't realize the importance of integrity and how its absence can adversely affect their kids. Imagine your child's goal is to learn how to play the guitar. However, if he practises for a few weeks, then slacks off, then picks it up for a few days, then slacks off again, the quality of his playing will be unpredictable. Now imagine that he has joined a band, and sometimes comes on time, and sometimes doesn't. The members would eventually be hesitant to keep him in the group, not knowing if he'd play properly that evening—or if he'd even show up to play at all. The same holds true for all types of activities: be it studying for maths, scoring on exams, performing in dramas, or even maintaining personal relationships.

Teach your children the importance of having integrity—of being consistent in what they think, what they say, and what they do. The fact is that the greater the unity among their thought processes and deeds, the greater their chances of finding success in each one of their pursuits in life.

Case study

In the course of running Jiva Public School, I found that many students were consistently coming late to school in the morning.

We instituted a zero-tolerance policy for being late. If a child is even one second late, he is sent home. At first, parents coming late with kids objected vehemently (especially the ones who showed up at times like 8:00:22). But, we adhered to our policy, and encouraged parents to bring their children 10 minutes earlier rather than 22 seconds later. Today, there are very few students who miss the 8:00 am mark, and I can be sure that after twelve years of learning this value, they will continue to be punctual in all aspects of their lives.

Taking failure in your stride

Part of building integrity is helping your children identify and overcome their inconsistencies. One challenge in doing so is that some children become sensitive when these shortcomings get pointed out. Such inadequacies are often termed as 'failures' in common performance scenarios.

Whenever a non-success occurs, explain to your children how to accept their sub-standard performance as a temporary situation that can be improved—not view it as a permanent characteristic of their personality. Remind them by saying: 'You are the person and not the activity. The *activity* was not a success. It doesn't mean *you* are not a success.'

Next, help your kids determine the genuine reasons for why they did not succeed. Assist them in investigating the problem and coming up with practical solutions as well as a plan that can help them improve their performance the next time round.

Ask them questions like:

- What went wrong?
- Was it lack of studying?
- Did you prepare well enough in advance?
- Were you just nervous?
- Were you distracted by something else?

This self-probing provides them with helpful feedback to improve their skills. It also wards against them looking for scapegoats or blaming external forces like the weather or others involved in the activity.

Case study

When I was leading a workshop for parents at Dum Duma Lake in Haryana, a young mother and father shared with me a concern about their daughter who was in Class 5. They explained that she was extremely disciplined and accomplished. She was also highly competitive, and had won numerous awards in all sorts of fields—painting, dancing, sports, and academics. However, she was unable to tolerate even a single word of criticism about her performance in any area.

I told them to start by asking her to critique her own self frequently, and find additional ways in which she could improve those areas. I then suggested that she should agree to listen to the criticism first without reacting, then go to another room to be alone for 10 or 15 minutes, and to ask herself to what degree she thought the criticism was valid.

Champions are courageous

In their lives, your children will inevitably have to face circumstances that are fearful, painful, risky, dangerous, or uncertain. They might find themselves lost from the group on a school trip, be called on to speak in front of a large audience without time to prepare, or be at the receiving end of a doctor's very long needle. It is at times like these that you hope they have enough courage to face the situations bravely.

Many parents love their children so much that they make every attempt to shield them from harm, and try to rescue or stand up for them. But, you will not always be there to protect your children. Therefore, it is important that you make every attempt to instil courage in your children. Teach your children the following ways to handle any situation with fortitude:

- **Teach them to believe in themselves:** Identify their natures, foster decision-making, and cultivate self-respect (Law no. 2).
- **Let them fight their own battles:** As long as they are not severely threatened emotionally or physically, let them stick up for themselves in arguments and confrontations.
- **Teaching them to think 'can do':** Remind them of the saying, 'If you think you can, you're right, and if you think you can't, you're also right.'
- **Encourage them not to shy away from competition:** Be sure they spend time playing some kind of competitive sports or games.
- **Don't make your home environment too safe:** If kids don't have exposure to knives, matches, electric wiring, etc., they will be more prone to injury when they discover them later on—especially, when you're not around.
- **Recall courageous people in trying times:** Encourage them to think what you or other courageous people would do in those situations.

- **Discourage negative self-talk:** Find out if they speak to themselves with self-deprecating statements like 'Oh, you're an idiot, how did you forget that', or 'I know I'm going to do poorly, I always do.' Get them to replace such words with positive statements like, 'You'll get it right next time', 'You're a champion', and so on.

Who does your child idolize?

Role models can provide a tremendous amount of motivation for children. Get your kids to identify people they look up to—who demonstrate excellence in their respective fields. Then have them put their pictures on their walls, read their biographies, watch movies on them, and so on. However, be sure to let kids know that heroes need not only be famous people who they see on TV. They can also be ordinary people who do extraordinary things. It could be a grandmother who lost her husband and raised the entire family by herself. Or, a neighbour who was visually impaired, but managed to complete his schooling and get a college degree. Further, get them to think of themselves as heroes in the making—training themselves to rise to the occasion in trying circumstances. Encourage them to remember their role models when they feel down and out, and to invoke their own heroic self to remind them of their super abilities. Talk with your kids about their idols. Ask them questions like: 'What qualities do they have?' 'How are you like or unlike them?' Involve grandparents and family members in the discussion. Have your children interview these people and ask them about the hardships they had to overcome in their lives.

Coaching tip: Music is a great motivator, especially in times of challenge. Have your children pick a motivational song that inspires them. Then, whenever they feel themselves losing heart, they can sing or recall that song. Examples could be 'Jai Ho' (from the film 'Slumdog Millionaire'), 'Allah Ke Bande' (by Kailash Kher), 'Hum Honge Kamyaab' (We Shall Overcome), 'I Won't Back Down' (by Johnny Cash) or the theme song from the film 'Rocky'. Make a list of motivational songs and convert it into a CD-ROM, a cassette, or a digital play list.

Case study

A mother contacted me about her nine year old son, Rajhans, who was being bullied by a student in his class. She had spoken to her son's teacher as well as the principal, but not much action was being taken. She was confused about whether to change her son's school or not.

I told the mother that she should only consider changing schools in the most extreme cases—that is, if the boy was in serious danger. I explained that the first thing she should do is to convince her son that he was not at fault in any way, and that he was deserving of respect. I told her to role-play with her son so he could practise what he would say to the other boy if he were bullied again. The woman emailed me back to tell me how surprised she was at her son's maturity of thinking, and how much more courageous he was than what she had expected. Much of the fear was her own. Within two weeks of this approach, the son was able to express himself skilfully enough before the other boy, who eventually stopped his intimidating behaviour.

Champions are adaptable

Colourful fish swimming in an aquarium are a wonderful sight. Yet, they are extremely sensitive and can die at the slightest fluctuation in water temperature or pH levels. Contrast that with fish in the rivers, seas and oceans that can easily withstand tremendous variations in water conditions. The reason is that the ones in the tank become so used to their controlled environment that they are incapable of coping with even minor changes to their settings. This situation brings to mind evolutionary theorist Charles Darwin's famous principle of 'survival of the fittest'. What most people don't realize, though, is that Darwin's definition of 'fit' did not refer to those who were the strongest or the fastest. It referred to the organism that was most *adaptable*, that is, one that could *change* the most quickly.

In addition to a focus on discipline, passion, integrity, and courage, a champion's training regimen should incorporate some lessons on adaptability. Find ways of pushing your children out of their comfort zones and into spaces they are less comfortable with. This will strengthen their ability to weather the difficult times and to acclimatize, whether it be a loss in family wealth, a death in the family, a need to suddenly shift localities, and so on. Here are ten things you can do to help your kids become more adaptable:

1. Send them on camping or hiking trips that require them to 'rough it out'.
2. Designate certain days as 'No TV' days.
3. Make your children travel by bicycle or bus even if you can afford to send them by car.
4. Have them participate in physically challenging sports.
5. Keep their allowance to a low, but reasonable amoun.
6. Let them learn how to repair basic things (sew a button, stitch a torn piece of clothing).
7. Make them find a bargain when shopping (don't just buy an item that's easily available, just out of convenience).
8. Encourage them to take responsibility for paper work (especially, things like admission forms, school loan applications, etc.).

9. Involve them in community service. (Cook and serve food at a local temple, help coordinate a blood donation camp, or assist a local Rotary or Lions Club with an outreach project).
10. Try growing some type of food (either through gardening or at a family village).

Interestingly, adaptation is directly linked to learning. In other words, those who can learn the fastest are able to adapt the fastest. So, by teaching your children to follow the 10 Laws of Learning, they will automatically learn to learn faster, and as such, adapt faster too.

Champions are detached

In the Bhagavad Gita, Arjun falls into a state of despair because he is forced to confront the opposing army which has many of his relatives, as well as his own guru. Lord Krishna, his charioteer and adviser, guides him by revealing the sacred truth that is at the core of this 5,000 year old classic: that one should perform one's karma without getting attached to the result.

It's important that we teach our children that not everything is in their hands. Simply put, you can't dictate what others will do. And sometimes, circumstances arise that are beyond our control. For instance, a flat tyre may prevent them from getting to the tennis match that they were destined to win, or the judge in an art competition who winds up being the aunt of one of the participants (who is ultimately awarded the prize despite her lacklustre performance). Explain to your children that all of us have our distinct natures, our duties, and our responsibilities. And when it comes to our efforts, we have to work with complete conviction to achieve our goals—because that's all we can do. All the rest is in the hands of fate.

I have seen that when people become too attached to the fruits of a particular type of labour, it takes a heavy toll on them when the desired result does not materialize. I know of children who were excellent at chess, but who became so dejected from not receiving a top prize that they dropped the game entirely. I know a man whose son was emotionally shattered because he did not achieve his dream of getting into an IIT, which he had been working towards for years. But, perhaps, worst of all are those who fail their board exams and are so heart-broken that they take their own lives. When I read the statistics that 16 children commit suicide *each day*, I became even more determined to reach out to parents to help their children keep things in perspective.

Coaching tip: Do not put too much pressure on your children when it comes to their studies. Teach them to give their best shot in everything they do. Success and failure are both part of life, like two teachers that work with us side by side to help us improve ourselves.

Be careful of awards

In 2003, I paid a visit to S. Ramakrishnan, a director in the Ministry of Information and Communication Technology (Government of India), and the person responsible for bringing the Internet into India. Ramki (as he is affectionately known by friends and colleagues) has one of the sharpest minds of anyone I've met. In the course of our conversation, as he was flipping through some of my new learning materials I had brought with me, I mentioned that my colleagues and I had recently won the World Summit Award for our work in e-health. Without looking up, he curtly replied, 'Be careful of awards,' and kept flipping the pages.

It was certainly not the response I expected. But at the same time, it was a profound comment that has stayed with me since. What I realized through this incident is how deeply attached people become to recognition and fame rather than to the actual work. I began to notice how some people pretended to be engaged in work only to win awards. This included professionals, but also students. In the process, I even noticed parents who would go out of their way to influence judges to ensure their children won prizes in contests. I also met children who became totally devastated if they lost competitions.

I'm not suggesting that you don't encourage your children to participate in events and win awards. I am only suggesting that the awards should not become the *main* motive for your child to do something. It is simply a bad practice as external motivators can be the worst type of motivators. They cause people to lose sight of the beauty, fun, and enjoyment of the activity itself, and can even tempt your children to use unfair means to win those awards. Worse, in future they might not do things if awards are not attached to them. So, make them understand that if they do things in the right way, accolades and success will automatically follow. In short, remember to teach your kids Ramki's words of wisdom: 'Be careful of awards.'

Champions are self-satisfied

Having grown up in America, I spent the first twenty two years of my life in an atmosphere that encouraged excess in everything. To buy new things even when the old ones worked just fine; to get a larger size soft drink or French fries, even when you knew you wouldn't be able to finish it; to buy a house that was so big that the one or two people living in it would feel like caretakers in an empty hotel. No one ever seemed satisfied with what they had. There was this constant feeling that until and unless you were onto bigger and better, whatever you had wasn't good enough. In October 2008, when the American economy collapsed, pundits agreed that the main cause for the downfall was unbridled, widespread greed.

One of the redeeming qualities that I found when I came to India was the value of being self-satisfied. I noticed that people tended to live more simply, were usually content with what they had, and were quite accommodating and generous. There was always more room in the car for another person, more space at the table for someone to eat.

If there is one champion quality you must teach your kids, it's to be self-satisfied. Help them find pleasure in the small things in life—working, cooking, cleaning, reading, spending time with family, stitching a button, or even repairing a broken iron. It will not only enable your children and family to maintain a balanced and harmonious existence, it will also teach your child the secret recipe of everlasting peace of mind.

> **Coaching tip:** Ensure that your kids count their blessings daily. Whenever they wake up, and/or whenever they go to bed, have them cup their hands a foot or two in front of their eyes. Using their hands as a 'screen', ask them to visualize all the things they have in their lives that they are grateful for. They can then fold their hands together and say a prayer of thanks.

Champions are compassionate

Once when I was in Mumbai, I was introduced to an affluent couple who had made a fortune from an IT company that the husband had built and then later sold. After having lunch at a fancy hotel, as we stepped outside, we were greeted by a polio-stricken pavement dweller. He approached us begging for money, walking on all fours because he was unable to stand upright. My male companion began to taunt the beggar, calling him 'dog boy' and shooing him away. The beggar followed us, scraping the bare flesh of his hands and knees along the pavement. The further we walked, the louder and more vicious the husband's abuses became. He eventually pulled a 50 rupee note out of his wallet and began to dangle it in the air above the beggar's head—just high enough so that the poor man couldn't reach it, making him 'perform' like a dog. After a few seconds he dropped the bill. Thoroughly disgusted, I said goodbye, knowing it was the last time I would ever speak to him. Days later, I found out that his twenty six year old son had committed suicide two months ago. In a way, I was not surprised, seeing how cruel and heartless this man was. So, teach your children that no matter how successful they become, their wealth is worth nothing if they cannot feel and heal the pain of others. Teach them that it is not something they should start doing once they are rich or less busy—there will never be enough money or enough free time. This should be a habit they should cultivate and practise regularly. Here are ten things you can do to make your child kind and compassionate:

1. Whenever your child gets a new toy or article of clothing, donate an old one.
2. Regularly have them perform social service such as teaching a child from the neighbourhood, giving food to those who are hungry, or taking care of a stray or injured animal.
3. Make them donate 10 percent of their allowance to a social cause.
4. Teach them to forgive someone who has done something wrong to them.
5. Encourage vegetarianism.
6. Have them do compassionate meditation, where they

concentrate on loved ones, and wish them well being and freedom from suffering.

7. Make them join a cause to help orphans, abused children, widows, the physically or mentally challenged, etc.
8. Teach them to be polite and avoid using abusive or threatening language.
9. Make them understand that by treating others with respect, they are actually earning respect for themselves.
10. Practise compassion not just for people, but for all living creatures. Avoid killing bugs and insects if possible. Don't throw rocks at stray animals.

Case study

A young couple from Uttar Pradesh came to me with their son who was in Class 2. They had another son who was thirteen years old and who was severely disabled with multiple sclerosis—it was so bad that the boy was unable to speak, walk, or even feed himself. The parents were extremely protective of the younger son, and tried to shield him as much as possible from his older brother, fearing he would be adversely affected by the elder sibling. They had finally reached a point where they were considering sending the younger son off to a boarding school.

After spending some time with the parents, I took the boy for a walk to have a chat with him and to find out what he thought of the whole situation. What surprised me was that he didn't seem to have an issue with his elder brother at all. In fact, he told me how he would sometimes 'exercise' him, read to him and play with him, and how much his brother loved him. When we returned to my office, I told his parents that they should let their younger son be at home. Instead, he should perform one type of service for his brother each day. It was my opinion that by sending him away, his heart might harden, and he might lose the connection with his sibling and his family. I then asked his parents the difficult question of who they thought would look their elder son after they were gone. The younger boy continues living with his family even today, happy to be with his elder brother.

Champions are respectful

In the film 'Lage Raho Munna Bhai', Sanjay Dutt plays the role of Munna Bhai, an underworld gangster who falls in love with Jhanvi, a popular radio jockey, and assumes the role of an expert on Mahatma Gandhi to get closer to her. In a scene in the movie, Munna Bhai joins Jhanvi on her show to provide advice to listeners on their relationship problems. When a girl calls up asking how she can know if a boy is 'the right one' for her, he responds by telling her to see how the boy behaves with service-class people. The scene then shifts to a restaurant where the young couple meet, and the boy speaks to her in the sweetest manner. But, when he turns his head to call the waiter over, he lets out a nasty hiss to get the latter's attention and summons him in a condescending, disrespectful way. When he turns back, the girl is gone.

You need to teach your children that everybody deserves respect, irrespective of class. Respecting family members, teachers, even others' work, no matter how small, goes a long way in earning good will and respect. In Law no. 2, we talked about how important it is to treat your children with respect—as that is the best place to begin.

An outgrowth of respect is gratitude, which is something you must also ensure you children develop. Whenever your children achieve something—good grades, a trophy for

Tae Kwon Do, or thunderous applause for their performance in the school drama, they need to realize that their success is partially due to the support they have received from others along the way. You can remind them of Sir Isaac Newton who when once praised for his remarkable accomplishments in the field of science, replied by saying, 'We stand on the shoulders of giants.'

> **Coaching tip:** Whenever you are recognized for your excellence (a job promotion, a beautifully cooked meal, a well organized family event) be sure to share it with your children.

Champions are enlightened

Help your children understand that there is a higher purpose in life, more important than just doing well in exams or getting into a top college. This is becoming a good human being. Get them to see that each one of us is acting out our roles, sometimes as children, parents, teachers, and so on, at different stages of our lives. As a champion, your child needs to understand the larger picture in life and give his best to each role in the eternal divine play or lila.

Teach them to be mindful

While topics of the divine may appear esoteric, there is a practical angle to enlightenment as well—and that is called 'being mindful'. Mindfulness refers to a state of complete awareness—aware of who you are, your relationship with others, what is going on in the world around you, what you should do in any given situation, and so on. Quite often, children do not succeed in their efforts because their minds are distracted. While they are studying for a test, they might start worrying about the future and what would happen if they fail. Or, after a poor dance performance, they might brood over the incident, inhibiting their concentration on the lecture their history teacher is currently giving. While they are eating, their minds might be completely absorbed in an action film, and because of their preoccupation with the story, they eat only half of what their body requires—or twice as much. Here are a number of tips you can follow to help your kids be more mindful:

- **Concentrate:** When they eat, they should concentrate on their food.
- **Listen actively:** When another person is speaking, they should stop all other activities and listen to what he or she is saying.
- **Use their 'Self-O-Meter':** Have them check in on themselves regularly to notice if they are hungry, thirsty, hot, tired, etc. (See Chapter 1, page 22.)
- **Avoid multitasking:** Don't try to do more than one thing at a time. Give each activity its due attention.
- **Slow down:** Don't feel a need to rush through things. Take your time and do them right.
- **Stop:** If things are getting overwhelming, stop what you are doing, take a deep breath, and get a fresh take on the situation.
- **Be present when you do any activity:** Use the 'be here now' technique if you find your mind wandering.

Short hand

- There is a difference between champions and winners. Winners may show temporary excellence, but champions demonstrate consistent profound qualities of character.
- Once your children have set clear goals and plans, work with them to stay disciplined and on the task to reach their targets. Help them keep their passions alive, and be there as a coach to cheer them on.

- Encourage your children to demonstrate consistency in their actions so their efforts take root. Help them identify their shortcomings to ensure their thoughts, words and actions are in alignment, and that they develop a reputation of being reliable and dependable.
- Champions need oodles of courage. So, take steps to build up their bravery reserves. While you teach them the virtues of positive self-talk and having a 'can do' attitude, you'll need to let them fight it out on their own sooner or later.
- Make sure that your kids are familiar with the virtues of adaptability, detachment, and self-satisfaction.
- Help them realize that champions need to be generous. They must respect others, demonstrate compassion for all living creatures, and recognize the value of being mindful.

Troubleshooting

1. Q: Our daughter does not eat green vegetables.
A: You need to help your daughter establish a relationship with vegetables. Take her shopping with you and let her pick out the vegetables herself. Let her carry them as well. Have her plan the menus with you and even help you a bit in preparing the food (even if it is a little thing like arranging the salad on a plate).

For additional tips, see Law 1: Take Care, p. 6.

2. Q: My six year old son is often irritable. He seems absent minded and tired most of the time.
A: He might not be getting enough rest. Ensure he gets at least 8.5–10 hours of sleep each night.
For additional tips, see Law 1: Take Care, p. 18.

3. Q: My teenaged daughter is extremely overweight. How do I get her to dump junk food?
A: Ensure that she avoids eating foods made with refined sugar and white flour (maida). See that she eats slowly, doesn't watch TV during meals, and that she meditates on her food while eating. Also, encourage her to do any type of physical exercise for at least 20 minutes everyday.
For additional tips, see Law 1: Take Care, p. 5.

4. Q: How do I know which career is best for my son?
A: Make your child take a Multiple Intelligence and Multiple Natures test. These will give you an indication of his aptitude and also suggest ideal jobs for his personality type. You can find such a test at www.jiva.com/careertest.

For additional tips, see Law 2: Believe in Themselves, p. 25.

5. *Q: My younger daughter is not as good in maths as my older daughter.*
A: Every child has eight Multiple Intelligences. Some of these are stronger than the others, and they vary greatly from individual to individual (even twins!) Please don't compare your daughters. Instead, find out your younger daughter's strong MIs (perhaps, Linguistic or Interpersonal Intelligence) and help her use those to her advantage.

For additional tips, see Law 2: Believe in Themselves, p. 25.

6. *Q: My son is extremely irresponsible. He never takes initiative to do things himself and is constantly dependent on others.*
A: Start giving him choices to build up his sense of independence. Let him choose what he'd like to eat, clothes he'd like to wear, order of activities in his daily schedule, etc.

For additional tips, see Law 2: Believe in Themselves, p. 33.

7. *Q: My daughter doesn't enjoy reading. How can I foster her interest in books?*
A: Ensure that she reads on topics that are of interest to her. Find out what she likes, and then accompany her to a bookstore or library and let her pick out books connected to those themes.

For additional tips, see Law 3: Explore, p. 49.

8. *Q: My son is not an original thinker. He hesitates when writing or drawing unless he's told specifically what to write or draw.*
A: Do fun exercises with him to develop his imagination and creativity. You can play the 'What if...' game (asking questions like 'What if there were no gravity?'), or the

'What do you get...' game (asking questions like 'What do you get when you cross a tree and a pair of pants?')

For additional tips, see Law 3: Explore, p. 56.

9. Q: I feel my daughter is lazy and somewhat aimless in life.

A: Ensure she has a list of goals. Have a goal-setting session with her and determine the areas that she would be interested to work on. Have her post that list on her bedroom wall, where she can see it at least twice a day—once when she wakes up and once when she goes to bed.

For additional tips, see Law 4: Goals, p. 64.

10. Q: My son sets out to achieve many things. But he is unable to fulfil most of what he says he'll do.

A: Often kids fail to achieve goals because the goals themselves are not clearly defined. Check that his goals are SMART (Specific, Measurable, Accurate, Realistic, and Time bound).

For additional tips, see Law 4: Goals, p. 66.

11. Q: I'm constantly chasing my children to finish their homework on time, but they seem to need constant prodding. How do I get them to do their homework on their own?

A: Ensure that they have a clear daily plan. Make it in the form of a timetable, with specific times and activities that begin from the time they wake up until the time they go to bed. And don't make it for them—have them make their routine chart themselves so that they feel a sense of ownership.

For additional tips, see Law 5: Plan, p. 73.

12. Q: My son is very careless. If you give him three things to do, he'll do one and forget the other two.

A: Have him keep a 'to-do' list. He can also keep a diary and list out all the things he needs to accomplish. As each task gets completed, let him cross it out, and move on to the next one. Whatever is not finished can be carried forward to the next day. Ensure he views the diary at least twice a day—before going to bed and after waking up.

For additional tips, see Law 5: Plan, p. 76.

13. Q: My children are glued to the TV all the time. What can I do?

A: Implement a set of TV Rules in your home. Limit TV time to no more than two hours per day. Ensure that your kids are not doing homework or eating while watching TV. Clearly spell out the consequences if the rules are breached and enforce them strictly.

For additional tips, see Law 6: Teach them the Rules, p. 88.

14. Q: Is it right for me to use incentives to get my daughter to do her homework and other chores that I need her to do?

A: No, using incentives is equivalent to bribing. In time, your child will begin asking, 'If I do that, what will you give me?' You can reward her when she has completed her work, but you should use this language, 'When you finish ___, you can__________', rather than 'If you do _________, I'll give you ___________'.

For additional tips, see Law 6: Teach them the Rules, p. 95.

15. Q: Is it alright if I beat my son sometimes for misbehaving?

A: No. If he is misbehaving so badly it is because of the environment you have created. Punishments are all right, but they should focus on a) getting your child to understand what he's done wrong, and b) making wrongs right (e.g., apologizing, fixing something he broke, paying for damages with allowance, etc.). Be sure punishments fit the crime, and be consistent with implementing them.

For additional tips, see Law 6: Teach them the Rules, p. 99.

16. Q: My daughter is unable to concentrate when she studies. She gets easily distracted.

A: Help create an effective 'Learning Zone' with her. Be sure to get rid of distractions by turning off the TV, computers, radios, etc. Also, ensure that she keeps a bottle of water nearby to stay well hydrated while studying.

For additional tips, see Law 7: Teach them to Practise, p. 106.

17. Q: My son is too restless and refuses to sit down to study for more than an hour.

A: Do not force your son to sit for hours doing nothing. Make a study session and study blocks with your son. For instance, have him create a single one hour study session that consists of three study blocks of 15 minutes each. He should also take 3–5 minute breaks between each block. Gradually, he can increase his study blocks to 20 minutes or longer, depending upon his capacity.

For additional tips, see Law 7: Teach them to Practise, p. 109.

18. Q: Whenever my son learns something new, he seems to forget almost everything by the next day.

A: Learning requires constant exposure. Ensure your son revises a new lesson within 24 hours of learning it. Also, make sure that he spends at least 50 percent of his study time only in revision.

For additional tips, see Law 7: Teach them to Practise, p. 112.

19. Q: My daughter gets extremely stressed out. She often feels overwhelmed by her syllabus, and ends up feeling depressed when she cannot cope up with it.
A: Ensure that she gets ample time to play. Play helps kids relax and makes them happy. It also helps them build physical, intellectual, and social skills that are critical for success in life.

For additional tips, see Law 8: Teach them to Play, p. 124.

20. Q: I want my children to have hobbies other than watching TV, but I can't seem to get them interested in anything else.
A: There are many activity ideas that you and your kids can choose from—many are free or cost very little money. These include learning musical instruments, magic tricks, reading, creative writing, bird-watching, gardening, cooking, origami, clay-modelling, and many more.

For additional tips, see Law 8: Teach them to Play, p. 127.

21. Q: My son finds it hard to remember so many facts and terms from his science and history syllabus.
A: Have him use memorization techniques such as acronyms and association. With acronyms, he can recall lists of words (e.g., VIBGYOR for the colours of the rainbow). With association, he can picture funny images along with the terms (e.g., Henle's Loop (a part of the kidney) can be remembered by a hen doing loops on a roller coaster and laying eggs (Hen Lays Loop).

For additional tips, see Law 9: Teach them the Tricks, p. 138.

22. Q: My daughter struggles with English, especially spellings.

A: Have her try breaking words into pieces (e.g., Feb-ru-ary, sat-is-fact-ion). She can also use more tactile techniques such as practising writing the words with her finger in the air, or spelling words with letter chits.

For additional tips, see Law 9: Teach them the Tricks, p. 140.

23. Q: *How can I tackle low self-confidence in my son?*
A: You can actually help him by not stepping in to save him when he needs help. Let him fight his own battles as far as possible. Promote a 'can-do' attitude by reminding him to avoid negative self-talk. Also, whenever he feels low, have him recall courageous people and think about what they would have done in a similar situation.

For additional tips, see Law 10: Perform like a Champion, p. 151.

24. Q: *My son is insensitive to others' feelings and sometimes displays a cruel streak. He lives in his own world and sees things only from his own perspective.*
A: Encourage him to be compassionate. Get him involved in some kind of social service—whether it be giving food to the hungry or taking care of stray animals. Have him donate 10 percent of his allowance to a social cause. You can also encourage him to practise vegetarianism or to forgive someone who has done something wrong to him.

For additional tips, see Law 10: Perform like a Champion, p. 159.

25. Q: *My daughter often fails to perform well on stage or in exams because at the critical moment, she loses her nerve.*

A: Have her practise 'being mindful'. Tell her to avoid multitasking, and to focus only on the task at hand. If she feels she is getting overwhelmed, tell her to slow down or stop what she's doing, take a deep breath, and then resume.

For additional tips, see Law 10: Perform like a Champion, p. 163.

Acknowledgements

I would like to thank the following people for making *The 10 Laws of Learning* happen.

Rishi Pal Chauhan for his inspiration and support for my work at every level. He is a rare person who embodies all the 10 Laws.

Lata Chauhan, Principal, Jiva Public School, who made students, teachers, and parents available to me during my research and writing of the book.

Satya Narayana Das for sharing his wisdom of Vedic knowledge that provided me key insights into each of the laws.

Dr Partap Chauhan for his valuable inputs on how children can take care of themselves with the help of Ayurveda.

Neerja Chauhan, who helped keep my schedule free at Jiva so that I could concentrate on writing.

Ranjit Sharma who helped with research and fact checking.

Bart Staub. My discussions with him inspired me to finalize the laws in their current form.

My brother, Jonathan Rudolph, who read early drafts of the outline and helped me crystalize the chapters on exploration and play.

My parents and grandparents who taught me by example and helped me understand the essence of the laws.

Meenakshi, Neerja, Madhusudan, Bharat, Ankita, and Aatman, who have been like my own children, and in whose upbringing I have been fortunate to participate and learn from.

Manbir Bedi of Primary Plus, who over the past two years has promoted my Laws of Learning workshops all over India, which have been critical in my research.

The teachers and mentors over the years who have inspired me, especially Angel Marcano, Robert E. Stueherk, and Rod Ellis.

My publisher Chiki Sarkar for giving me this opportunity and my editor Milee Ashwarya for her critical eye in editing and restructuring the content in a way that has significantly improved its flow.

Finally, my thanks to the many parents, children, teachers, and principals I have worked with over the years, who have provided me with the knowledge and insights that have culminated in this work.

A Note on the Author

Steven Rudolph is an American educationist, researcher, TV personality, and public speaker based in India. In 1994, he introduced the Internet to Indian schools and followed it up with the first series of constructivist computer textbooks for Indian children. As Educational Director of Jiva Institute and founder of Jiva Public School, he has developed many innovative learning materials for students to help them realize their potential. He is the proponent of a novel concept in education called 'Multiple Natures' that is used to help individuals identify careers that are compatible with their personality types. Rudolph is a popular face on TV, notable for his show *Discover your Child,* on the *Care World* Channel and *Zee Jaagran*, where he addresses parenting issues. He is also widely known for his unique life-skills workshops that have been attended by thousands of children, parents, and teachers throughout the country. Rudolph has served as a consultant to the World Bank, UNESCO, the Department of Human Resource Development (Government of India), the NCERT, the CBSE, the ICSE, and companies including Apple Computer, Microsoft, Intel, HP, and Wipro. He holds a masters degree in education from Temple University.